THE NAKED TRUTH

Win or Learn

20/20 VISION PRESS

Authors: Christine Beckwith, Elizabeth Karwowski

Editor and Compiler: CaZ (Candy Zulkosky)

Additional Authors / Contributors:

Patty Arvielo	Marcia Griffin
Ginger Bell	Kim Hoffman
Laura Brandao	Regina Lowrie
Karen Deis	Mary Ann McGarry
Jen Du Plessis	Maria Vergara
Cindy Ertman	Sue Woodard

Win or Learn / Christine Beckwith and Elizabeth Karwowski
First edition / 20/20 Vision Press

ISBN 978-1-954036-01-7

Contents

— DEDICATION —

Does anyone ever read Dedications? I do. And I hope you do.

This book is dedicated to you if you are a woman. It is dedicated to you if you support a woman in pursuit of happiness and dreams.

Most of all it is dedicated to every little girl who dreams of success in life yet to be defined.

Chapter 1

Why This Book?

Life is full of lessons disguised as heartache, disruption, and downfalls. We do not always pull a seat up to the table with pen in hand to receive them. Sometimes lessons come in hindsight or after we recover from a break or the occurrence of tragedy. The collective voices in the pages of this powerful book are raised to tell the stories and share the hard-won lessons of 14 women whose careers in the finance industry span decades. The roads they traveled, while often parallel, inevitably entwine and wind in an ebb and flow as they have each risen to their own professional peaks.

Each has endured triumphs and tribulations in their long journey to success. Each has ultimately grown from the lessons learned both in the moment and in hindsight. Today they are the leaders in the mortgage finance space; powerful, experienced, and important role models, garnering respect across the industry. Each takes this responsibility seriously while embracing the real and fun and human side of themselves.

The stories in this book are shared by women who are powerful in the boardroom, control millions, and remain fully able to place tongue in cheek to present a serious message with humor and love. The *Naked Truth* promised on the cover and in the book's subtitle is reinforced in each chapter you read.

For the first time, these collective voices are raised to honor the path taken, laugh at the stories, and teach the lessons of a complex profession. These voices have come together from an idea Elizabeth Karwowski, executive leader and CEO of her own firm, brought to Christine Beckwith, 30-year plus industry veteran and founder of a premiere coaching company.

"When Elizabeth approached me in a phone conversation," Beckwith shares, "I had no intention on writing another book right now, having released three best sellers in the past 28 months. I instantly realized the collective power of this book and could not resist being a part of bringing these amazing stories to the world." ~ Beckwith

These 14 leaders built their careers during an era where advocacy was incredibly quiet, often facing heightened discrimination and diminishment. Yet, a book pointing fingers at any one race, ethnicity, gender, or place or spewing hate and resentment was never considered.

These women have come together simply to leave their mark in history and pay forward to the next generation of leaders.

"For me, this day is surreal. Living in a time where we can openly talk about our misgivings and our hurt or our lessons is, in and of itself, remarkable. I am grateful the silent and lonely years have passed. I know I speak for all the authors when I say our wish is to gift the world a message of hope, resilience, gratitude, grace, fire, and fierceness to forge forward and conquer your dreams." ~Beckwith

It is the hope of this collective for readers who buy our book to see the honor, the lessons, and the humor we put into sharing our journeys. We realize we are not a famous group of people even though our names are recognized in our industry as leaders, speakers, teachers, and influencers. Our stories are different and our paths diverse. Our message is unified and introduced clearly here by Christine Beckwith:

*"When I think of **Win to Learn,** and the core of the women represented here, I am reminded of my great aunts, Iris Frechette and Fern Stiles. My grandfather's two older sisters represented an era of woman I find beautiful. They were homemakers and literary*

contributors. One kept the history of our family and the other one kept our family legacy alive in her interactions by storytelling our families history. One was a wife and the other a maid never married.

Fern was a librarian. Both were salt-of-the-earth women; hardworking. At Fern's funeral, a man stood in the congregation to share a memory of giving her a ride on his snowmobile to the general store when she was well into her 80s, during the harsh winters of the great northern woods in New Hampshire.

We are meant to be literary contributors and storytellers. I know this is not a gender trait, as of course I see the incredible male writers and authors of our times. Even so, to write an industry book of lessons is more likely to have occurred in our camp than anywhere else. I am proud to carry the torch of my great aunts' mindsets.

I have two rocking chairs in my counseling studio, one from my great grandmother and the other belonged to Aunt Fern. I sit in those chairs at times of solitude to think. They are calming and comforting. I imagine myself handing those chairs down one day to an unknown younger generation yet to be born.

I see the same future for this book being handed down to generations coming up who want to navigate the waters of their careers."

Life lessons are extremely hard to assess while one is amid the lesson. When viewed in real time, the reason for the hardship, the positive to perhaps come out of it, is never easily apparent.

HINDSIGHT CLARIFIES FOCUS.

This book is filled with clear visions built from hindsight and experience. Our hope is to see these lessons embraced by the leaders behind us and be used to navigate past and through roadblocks in their own careers. This book, written and compiled during an historic pandemic has, and will, change lives, change views, and awaken perspectives.

Win or Learn: The Naked Truth is our gift, an unearthing of words and wisdom, and the sharing of a wealth of experience.

Here's to Winning AND Learning!

Chapter 2

Call Me Crazy

Christine Beckwith

I am not sure where I was when I first contemplated whether I had lost my mind (or not). It became a recurring thought over three decades. It would come without warning, a ghost of a feeling lingering in a space not visible or clear. A certainty something had just happened. It felt horrible and yet I was left with no proof of wrongdoing. No proof of deliberate slight. Simply a surety of wrongness.

I have come to know this to be a common sentiment and feeling, an experience described by many people when dealing with someone who is subtly manipulating one's environment, perhaps even initiating difficult to pin down passive-aggressive behavior.

Recognizing you are a target for this action, sorting out the reasons why, determining if it is real or if you are imagining it, can be the most difficult part. Truly, I think it takes time, keen eyesight, and a certain amount of intuitiveness to see the pattern without becoming paranoid. I have helped hundreds of people sort through experiences like this, and I have become a sharp protector in my own life when I recognize it happening.

One of my clearest memories of this happened in a board room populated by myself and about 12 men. I had a suggestion, which was literally dismissed and met with silence from the entire room, only to hear ten minutes later the same suggestion made by someone else. As the entire table erupted in loud agreement, I remember wondering, *"Am I invisible right now?"*

I have heard comedians call this mansplaining. It is not funny. I mean, it is comic. We identify with it and because laughter is medicine, we laugh about discrimination which has plagued us our whole careers. Still, it is not funny.

I have seen this practice used many times against others. I remember being part of a pool of six people with one female leader. I estimate there was a 10 percent approval of the senior female leader's ideas. I personally thought she was brilliant. I could also see she was strong, and herein lies the real issue. To acknowledge a strong woman is emasculating to narcissists. I have watched it my entire career. They will not admit a woman is on the right track if in the process it means they feel less. This thinking is a deeply embedded form of discrimination.

What is our defense against such commentary by discriminators? Are our ideas, visions, plans, and projects being rejected for legitimate reasons sweeping the discrimination under the proverbial carpet? Where does this leave us when our voice is silenced, when we are ignored, and when our ideas are squashed? What if the leader over us is blatantly discriminating against us?

Another time I experienced pay inequality when a manager offered a salary plan I knew paid me less for more work. When I balked, he told me to track it for six months and if I was paid less to come back and make a good argument.

Let this sink in for a moment.

Take less money for more work for a period of six months and then argue for your return to same or better pay? Really?

You might be surprised to know I went along with his demeaning suggestion. I did what he asked. Six months later, on the eve before I turned in my spreadsheet evidence showing the drop in my pay, I gave him a heads up. What ensued was a painful, enduring battle. It was also Machiavellian devious. He chose to simply not assist me in my duties. Rather, he subtly impeded my efforts throughout our entire work process. Eventually, he took a misstep. He made a threat (there was proof of the threat), and he was extracted from all future negotiations.

Sometimes I sit in awe of that time, reflecting on what I went through, even though it remains hard for me to revisit such a stress-filled time. People who have experienced this kind of treachery know how demeaning it can be. I could cite more examples of his discrimination. The situation didn't improve for me. Over time, I found myself relegated to the bottom of agendas, overlooked, blatantly talked about behind my back, and aggressively bullied. My only choice in dealing with this was to stand up to it and decide if I could live with the aftermath.

Of course, my inner self wanted peace. I had not asked for this to happen to me. I wanted my work to stand for itself. My work was my voice. I wanted my results to shine as a beacon and marquis, as they always had. Sadly, during this chapter in my career story, I could not be that person, and this is where the lesson comes into focus.

I found myself in uncharted waters in my career and life. I had done incredible work; I had risen consistently through the ranks. I had earned the respect of the employees who worked for me and with me. In truth, the bond I created with many coworkers saw me through this terribly difficult intersection.

The outcome, if we speed ahead, was my resignation and exiting a job I loved in an act of self-preservation. This was no firm, certain walk to the door. I truly felt unsure every step of the way. Yet even in uncertainty, I had a vision, an invisible strength I could draw upon to guide me.

Today I have turned past heartache into lessons recorded in my curriculum. For example, Pay Negotiation, a course taught from a female leader's perspective, is chock-full of strategy and defense against diminishment and the kind of treatment I experienced.

Being in a horrible work situation is a difficult intersection. When do we decide our happiness and integrity mean more than our work environment? We may decide to leave money, honor, power, prestige, and even friendships and community—all because of one bad person. One person who does not act with integrity, who makes life miserable, who is intimidated and feels threatened by a power we may not even realize we hold.

What motivates a person to cause angst? Is it jealousy? Fear? I believe it is a lack, an emptiness inside, a hole the person wants to fill by stealing power they could never possess due to their own lack in emotionally intelligent areas.

BROKEN SPIRIT!

To break the spirit of a person like me, one cannot just poke me in the shoulder. It has happened plenty of times and without flinching I have prevailed. I have had my spirit broken slowly and methodically. It felt like a tide inexorably rolling in each day, tearing jagged edges in my psyche by subtle, repetitive blows. Slowly, but surely, I have been worn down to the point where every day I felt pure exhaustion.

Misery became my normal existence. I felt hurt by those who were not coming to save me, my colleagues who could see what was happening and chose to stand on the side, blatantly silent. I could not understand how dedicated service was not enough. There were moments I felt betrayed as I realized no one was coming to save me.

In the end there would be a few good people left standing at my side; incredibly strong people who, despite my imposed unpopularity, despite the imminent threat of retribution, kept me from being alone at the lowest moments of a horrendous time.

There are clichés written about intersections such as these in life. Even at my lowest, I knew I was not alone in strife. And yet, even in that knowledge, there were times I was broken. I would rise each day and follow the same routine, one devoid of internal hope and excitement. I would think hard during my morning exercise about what could be thrown at me. My guard was up continually.

Sadly, I was not the single target. I witnessed others facing the same horror. Some experienced even more egregious wrongdoings. I was helpless to stop any of it. I felt a fraud. I felt like the advocate and leader I was lauded to be, I was no longer. I was shrinking. I was a wilting flower. I was, without question, dying inside.

TERMINAL BUSINESS ILLNESS

I share how I feel while this was happening because too often we talk about the act, the defense, and the solution, but not the trauma the entire experience causes. Show me a person who dedicates themselves wholly to a job, a warrior who cares about the people, who shows up for all the meetings, who goes to war with and for the company, and you're showing me a person whose emotional tie is typically unbreakable. To bring the person to a place where they want to leave is like setting the building on fire and watching them jump out the window. It is not easy to witness. Most people realize when this happens something went terribly wrong.

LETTING THE LIGHT IN!

The antagonist in this story was not taken out. I could not take him out, even though he should have been taken out. That reality was life changing. It took years of therapy and coaching to unpack what happened to me.

Trauma is a real thing. When everything you believe in is shattered and your reality becomes elusive, when evil wins over good and you know in your heart your reality is wrong, it causes you to question everything around you. This time in my career made me question my own value system. Had I placed too much emphasis on my work? Had I given too much of myself to this company? I asked myself, *why is this situation destroying me?*

I CHOSE TO GET OFF THE TRAIN.

I am certain, even as I write this, my departure was a painful and harsh reality for my subordinates. Our environment had been made toxic by the perpetrator who, by his continued survival, touted victory. The troops were my greatest fans. I am certain they knew there were unspoken reasons for my departure.

No one will ever know how alone and difficult my final walk to the door was. And yet, I took only one night to sit with my sadness before beginning the necessary swim toward a new shore.

I cannot forget, and must repeat my thanks for, the people who swam with me; people who kept watch to ensure I made it to safe ground. When I looked around there were fewer people in my peripheral but those who remained were strong. I believe I helped others find their own lessons in my act of survival and perseverance. I was once again the protagonist in my own story.

It is difficult to act with emotional intelligence in the heat of battle. The experts say to remain calm. I teach this tactic today as a coach.

I stand today on a new shore with many life-enhancing, changing, and strengthening lessons formed by this and other experiences. In truth, there were losses for me in choosing to take a stand against this unjust treatment. In hindsight, my return on investment for making this move is surprisingly positive. The emotional losses I experienced were immediately replaced by joy and happiness and eventually a financial ROI followed.

Did I lose? The answer depends on how you measure losses.

This was one pivotal event amid many in my career. My story is still being told. In matters both personal and financial, I am coming out on top. Where we measure the important currencies in life, I have won. I am an example. I am sought out by those who see strength and value honesty and integrity.

In every person's story there is a chapter where we decide to go all in or to lose it all. I know few people would have made my choice. I believe there are thousands, sadly perhaps millions, of women who are diminished, discriminated against, and sexually harassed, who are unhappy and miserable working every day. They tell themselves their incomes are lifelines and their careers cannot withstand a fight-back narrative, and perhaps this is, in fact, their story. Perhaps these millions of women who work for less than their counterparts, who are not promoted, who aren't being heard, and who turn a blind eye to wrongdoing out of fear of retribution are living a true story. In every person's story, the page turns. A new chapter can and will be written.

I have earned my way to incredible income. I have found internal strength I never had before. I am more honest than I have ever been. I have proven to myself I am a person of extraordinarily deep integrity.

I saved myself and have since experienced more success than I imagined. There is a strength living deep inside my core. Finding the strength has gifted me with the realization I am a morally sound human being. This gift alone has set me on a course where the ROI is immense. We often wonder what we would do in a situation where truth is required but unpopular. I do not wonder any longer.

I have written three best-selling and award-winning books. I have been the subject of dozens of national awards. I have become a columnist in national industry magazines. I have stood on enormous stages to share my wisdom and my excellence as a leader and today I am helping thousands of professionals build better businesses in our field. The handcuffs are off. I am my own boss; my light shines brightly, and everyone sees it.

I took back the freedom I lost, the heartbreak I endured, and I turned jaded bitter energy into a mountain of positivity. I have written more than 50 business courses. I have built one of the largest coaching firms in the nation and I have the fastest growing women's business coaching firm in America.

Adversity will strengthen you. Hurt will shape you. Breaks let in the light. I catch myself staring at my life wondering how I got here. This was a vision I had for the future, never intended for now. I am a person of strong faith and it is God who sat with me in my lonely moments. I know He had a hand in this.

I have made peace with this story and others in my past. I have forgiven wrongdoing. I have forgiven those who did not save me.

Yet, I have not forgotten nor will I ever.

There are hundreds of people who I served as their faithful leader over my entire career, who I left behind each time I moved to the next chapter in my life, and who continue to follow me. I believe they have witnessed my strength. They know what my heart is about, what I stand for, and they show up to cheer me on. They come to the audiences of my conferences, they post and comment on the public social media waves. They are still there, and they still call me in hardships and times of need, and I still desire to take their calls and be their mentor.

My greatest lesson is you can change the title and the money, but you don't lose the power. The titles do not matter. When people say you are their leader, then you are. In the end I found what matters most to me. I live to serve, and I do so, with all my heart. This bond and commitment fuels my success today and propels us into the future at high velocity.

I have forgiveness in my heart for people and things so I can embrace peace in my life. I have learned holding on to past wrongdoing depletes you and changes you if you let it.

My lessons are still coming. All humans seek education and lessons and over time the wisdom we gain allows us to understand when and why events happen, how our paths turned ever so slightly or hugely in a new direction, and where greater happiness and love can be found.

I believe I am exactly where I am supposed to be today and this gives me great joy and comfort. I vow, for the remainder of my life, I will continue to share these lessons for all who want to hear them.

We never lose! We only learn!

ABOUT THE AUTHOR

Christine Beckwith

CHRISTINE (BUFFY) BECKWITH is an Award-Winning, Executive Sales Leader who has spent 30 years in the mortgage finance industry. Her life and career are the culmination success stories reaching all the way back to her childhood. A Best-Selling and Award-Winning Author, Christine branched out in 2018 to begin her dream job as the Founder and President of 20/20 Vision for Success Coaching and Consulting.

After breaking many glass ceilings in the mortgage and banking industry, Christine is a columnist for magazines and is a special correspondent anchoring the news and interviewing experts in her industry. She is the publisher of a successful industry-themed duo of magazines and an advocate for women, dedicating a complete division in her own company to the cause amongst many causes and communities she touches at a vast level.

Christine is active on the national speaking circuit lecturing on topics including her expertise in finance and sharing her personal stories of inspiration and motivation while delivering both tactical and practical advice. Over the span of Christine's 30-year career, she consistently ranked in the top 5 percent of the respective sales teams beginning with her years as an originator all the way through the sales ranks in many layers of branch, eventually reaching regional then senior leadership roles. She has been coined by MPA Magazine, "The Gordon Ramsey of Banking Coaches" for her ability to take companies and teams to superior financial success.

Breaking mainstream in 2019, Christine has appeared on huge stages to speak, kicking off the year at the Miami Garden Stadium with Gary Vaynerchuk Agent2021 as the "Real Estate Expert Panel" Moderator. She has spoken at the Anaheim Convention Center in Los Angeles, The Hard Rock Casino in Atlantic City, NJ, and for numerous prestigious organizations and media companies.

Christine will tell you writing, teaching, and speaking are at the core of who she is, enabling her legacy work with a commitment to make a difference in the lives of professionals and youth everywhere.

Christine is a mother, a girlfriend, a daughter, a sister, an aunt, a homemaker, and a lover of laughter, good health, and home and heritage. She calls herself "a happy human."

Chapter 3

Breaking Bad

Lessons Learned on the Road from
Breakdown to Breakthrough

Sue Woodard

*"That little girl is so tenacious, if you
asked her to go pick up that garage
and move it over three inches, she
might not be able to move it, but she'd
go give it her best shot. And heck, she
might even do it." ~ My dad, circa 1972*

This is one of my earliest memories. I was
three or four years old, sitting in a red booster
chair in my grandmother's kitchen in Marietta, Georgia.
When I heard my dad say this, my little heart lit up with

pride. Sure enough, persistence has served me quite well throughout my life, helping me reach personal and professional goals beyond the dreams of the little girl in the booster chair.

Aww, how sweet, right?

There is another side to consider. My tenacity and ability to stick with something, no matter what, has also caused episodes of what I call breaking bad. For fans of the television network drama, you may now be envisioning me in an RV, cooking meth out in the desert. Breaking bad means something a bit different to me. It's how I describe the times I tenaciously hung onto something far too long before making a needed change, ultimately hitting a wall, and suffering a breakdown of some sort before I reached a breakthrough.

Being tenacious does not mean I always win the battle. I have had wins and losses and have stories to share, complete with lessons learned along the way, helping me avoid the painful breakdowns and moving more quickly on my way to powerful breakthroughs.

What counts as a breakthrough? Think of something in your life you once thought was impossible, and now it is in your life. Achieving your *something impossible* was a breakthrough. A breakthrough is the act of moving through or beyond an obstacle (and notice the word act).

A breakthrough can be relatively small like waking up earlier every day, learning to play the ukulele, or making a connection with someone you've always wanted to meet. A breakthrough can be big like standing up in front of a crowd to give a speech, starting a new business, or moving across the country. A breakthrough is when you take a decisive action or series of actions because you want something in your life to change.

A breakthrough is a moment in time when the impossible becomes possible.

There are times a breakthrough happens because it was preceded by a breakdown—a malfunction, failure, crash, collapse, or disintegration. It is during the breakdown when breaking bad comes into play, with a wake-up call so severe and painful you are propelled to embrace the actions you knew all along you needed to take.

Sometimes things must fall apart so they can then fall together. A break is not always avoidable. I have learned this lesson well: if I can make a decision and take an action more quickly and avoid breaking bad—particularly when the break may impact someone else I care about—then I surely want to learn to do things differently, wouldn't you? It all starts with simple, basic procrastination.

When I was asked to contribute to this book project, I was honored and delighted. This amazing group of women met with an accomplished editor, we outlined the plan, and later the same night, I sat right down and went to work. I finished my chapter in less than a week, surprising and delighting all involved.

Lies, all lies.

This absolutely did not happen. I procrastinated past the deadlines to the consternation of all, and thankfully made it under the wire.

Ever do anything like this? And does it surprise you about me? So why does this happen?

Often, we look at successful people and see only their public state without considering what goes into making the sausage. The backstage reality isn't always pretty. Too often, the hard work behind the scenes is portrayed like one of those classic scenes from a glamorous movie, going from unenlightened dummy to successful superstar with a cool montage of whiteboards, late-night flights, laptops, and high fives, all set to an amazing soundtrack. Progress is frequently ugly, slow, and loaded with failures. A breaking-bad event is often what finally propels action to move forward, even when experiencing trauma or failure causes us to step back, re-evaluate our deepest motivations and decision-making process, and reflect on whether our strategies are working well or not.

I find it interesting (and revealing) when we apply this concept to the mortgage industry. In 2008, there was a terrible crash. I would surely call the widescale event during that time a breakdown of the mortgage industry—and frankly the whole financial universe we operate in. Evidently it needed to happen because change was not coming fast enough. We could feel things were not quite right. There was a definitive breakdown, followed by a breakthrough, resulting in a new way of doing business. In recent years, more examples have risen, fortunately not preceded by a breakdown. It can be seen when we consider the changes in customer experience, in digital innovation, and in technology advancement, all of which led to breakthroughs.

Consider what we want in our business and our life. We generally know when a change is needed because we feel it and we want it. Generally, we even know what is needed to achieve the change. We can Google it, we can buy 20 books, we can cyber stalk people who are doing it successfully. We want the change. We see the change. We know it's in reach. Why don't we have it already? Why is it hard to do what you know will improve your business, your relationships, your health, and your life? Why do we become trapped in this gap between knowing and acting? It truly is a knowledge-action gap. We know what to do, but we cannot seem to do it.

The solution is simple—but not easy. It requires a bit of force on our part because there's a whole lot of force working against us. I know this force. I put the *pro* in procrastination. I have intimate knowledge of this gap that appears insurmountable at times.

I have come to believe there are depths of procrastination. There is a normal, garden variety procrastination where we innocently scroll through social media and before we know it, two hours have passed while we have been in tears watching dogs greet their owners coming home from deployment, watching videos of cats being cats, or accidentally delving into deep research about whether weasels can survive in the Arctic. (Side note—they can.) We eventually do the laundry because we run out of clothes. We finish paying the bills because they are due. We finish the draft of the chapter because otherwise we can't be in the book.

To varying degrees, everyone is guilty of this innocent procrastination. It is frustrating, yet we manage to move forward—because deadlines are involved, and a bit of panic comes on the scene to help propel us.

Going a layer down, there's a deeper, darker level of procrastination where forces hold us back and keep us from making the changes we know need to be made.

This level of procrastination pops up often when no specific deadlines are involved. It pops up when we have a desire, a real desire, to accomplish or change something profoundly important. For example, perhaps there's a relationship we need to end. Maybe it's time to focus on improving health. Maybe there's a career change needed. Suddenly there's a lull in our world, there's no looming deadline, and yet we are stopped dead in our tracks. An invisible force is holding us back.

When this deep procrastination happens, it can be damaging. This is not resolved by putting down the phone to regain a few hours lost to social media. When the forces in our life bring this level of procrastination to bear, it is necessary to take a step back to examine life. It could be you have dropped back so far as to be almost a spectator in your own life. It could be you've stopped driving the car; you've hitched a ride going somewhere you don't necessarily want to go. This intersection is where a breakdown can happen. I've experienced this, and I suspect, without giving it a name, so have you.

Why does a breakdown occur? There are many reasons. Here are a few which may be familiar and have the ring of truth to you, as they do to me.

INERTIA

I believe inertia is the most powerful force in the world. Inertia is what keeps our plans, desperately wanted hopes, and even the unexpected from falling into our laps and magically happening. Remember the ab belts advertised on late-night television? The one with the electrodes? The promise was to build rock hard abs by strapping on a belt sending electric pulses to your ab muscles. The appeal was having the ability to hang out and watch TV and develop rock hard abs. Crazy, right? Of course, I bought one. Of course, I did not gain rock hard abs. Inertia. Matter at rest remains at rest unless acted upon by an external force.

How often do you go to bed on a Sunday night and think, "Tomorrow it's the new me! I'm going to wake up early, journal, meditate, go to the gym, and be at the office by 6:30 a.m. I'll accomplish amazing things!" In the morning, you wake up, hit the snooze button, and say, "Forget it. Maybe tomorrow."

We all have an internal snooze button. We have amazing ideas about things we could do, and we don't do them. We hit our internal snooze button because we don't feel like doing it. Here's a truth to embrace; in any area of life where we want to see a breakthrough or change, we are never going to feel like doing what it takes to accomplish it! Inertia says it's easier to do nothing. It's easier to only do the fun stuff.

In the long run, outcomes requiring effort are the most meaningful. Running a marathon makes us happier than eating chocolate cake. Being a great parent makes us happier than beating a video game. Growing our business makes us happier than watching cat videos.

And there's a weird corollary to inertia. (Maybe it's ertia?) It shows up when we can't work on our important project because we are very, very busy. While writing this chapter, my inbox was cleaner than ever. My sock drawer was sorted by color and function. My fridge had not one expired item in it. I found myself becoming super productive and focused on non-essentials. When a big task looms, we know we are procrastinating when we falsely find ways to be busy. Focusing on the wrong tasks might feel good in the moment, but it's feeding inertia and does not accomplish the bigger goals.

SUBCONSCIOUS SABOTAGE

Our subconscious mind powers 95 percent of our brain. It is designed to stop us from doing anything hurtful. Sabotage starts with something subtle, a natural action. Typically, most of us hesitate before we act. During the moment of hesitation, your brain wakes up and says, "Whoa there! We're doing something out of the norm. Something must be up, and I need to protect her by stopping this urge to take action." On some level, we briefly feel better when we step back and don't take the action.

ACTUAL DEFICITS

There could be a true challenge holding us back leading to breakdown. If so, the interruption must be dealt with to achieve breakthrough. Maybe we don't have the skill or the tool to proceed. Maybe it's one of the reasons you're holding this book; you might benefit from coaching, researching, and learning. We must stand on the shoulders of those who went before. We will see better and farther. By learning from what has already been done, we take faster steps towards what hasn't. There is no shortage of ideas. There is a shortage of people who act on them.

Perfectionism

Perfectionism is a dangerous state of mind in an imperfect world. We are imperfect people living imperfect lives. The drive and desire to make something perfect is one of the biggest causes for never starting. This is a real danger. Striving for perfection is a worthy cause! Focusing too tightly on being perfect is like carrying a 200-pound shield you think will protect when it weighs you down and holds you back.

The truth is (and we all know this) nothing is perfect. Nothing. What I've learned is people don't care as much about what WE are doing and how perfect it is as we think they do. People are way too busy thinking about themselves. I was in this zone of perfection once, obsessing over something I was working on and what people would think of it, think of me. A dear friend said to me, "You know, you're pretty funny. Do you really believe people are thinking about you that much? They aren't. Get over yourself." And she was right!

Even when we make a massive mistake, people move on far more easily than we do because they're obsessing about their own mistakes! Frankly, perfection is boring. Your true unvarnished self is what people want. Exercise tolerance toward your own quirks and shortcomings, and you'll grow in courage and resilience.

Pain avoidance

Interestingly, pain is biologically helpful and protects us. Pain teaches us not to put our hand into a fire or to take a huge gulp of delicious coffee without temp testing it first. Life has all kinds of pain in it. The question isn't what you want to enjoy—most of us would easily give similar answers to that question. The more important question is, *"What pain are you willing to sustain and for what purpose will you endure pain?"*

Most people want big financial success. Not everyone is willing to deal with insane hours, long commutes, obnoxious paperwork, and everlasting work weeks—all of which may be required. Everyone wants a great relationship. Not everyone is willing to go through tough conversations, awkward silences, hurt feelings, and compromises that are typically part and parcel. Everyone wants a great physique. Unless we embrace the pain of going to the gym regularly, we won't achieve it.

The pain of staying in our current state must become greater than the pain of making the change, taking the action, and having the breakthrough. Breakthroughs often arrive when we find ourselves quietly realizing the choice is between two pains: the pain of the jump or the pain of regret. Change is not comfortable; sometimes it is downright painful. We can choose change, or we can choose comfort. We cannot have both.

FEAR

Fear comes in all sizes and colors. Fears can grip us and keep us from acting. Fear is an internal voice that grows in volume, asking, *"What if I'm not good enough? What if they laugh at me? What if I'm rejected? What if I'm found out as not being as smart as they think? What if I'm misunderstood? What if I am a disappointment? What if I fail?*

What if?" Fear can absolutely grip us and keep us paralyzed—unless we shift our relationship with fear.

I had a mortal fear of public speaking. For years, my presence on a stage was closely preceded by me tossing my cookies behind the stage. Why would I, or anyone, be afraid of speaking in front of a group? I was afraid of being judged. And you know what? I was judged. Amazingly, I discovered it didn't kill me. It motivated me. It made me stronger and I am glad I didn't give up.

Fear is a tough challenge for most of us. One of the best methods I know to overcome fear is to replace it with something we are even more afraid of. Become more afraid of reaching the end of your life and realizing there are many things yet to do, to say, to share, to become. Fear quickly takes a backseat to acting when we think in terms of the impact of NOT acting.

A quick side note related to emotions because fear is certainly a powerful emotion: When we are fearful, overwhelmed, and embarrassed, the easy path is to check out and push off decisions. Worse yet, it is easy to make bad decisions when fear is involved. Don't call your parents. Don't schedule the meeting. Skip the workout. Eat unhealthily. Hit the snooze button three times, or four, or more.

Emotions are not a choice. Actions are. Have you ever been told to stop being angry or stop being sad? Of course. We all hear it and probably all say it. Yet it's like telling someone to stop being diabetic. It's ridiculous advice. We cannot help having emotions. We cannot stop emotions from arriving. We are human.

Yet we can control our actions, our words, and our behaviors. Emotions are the result of our mind comparing our environment with our expectations. Quite often, reality and expectation are not in sync. It is totally OK to have and feel negative emotions like anger or fear. They can be helpful. When emotions take control and drive our actions—or more to the point our inaction, we are ultimately the less for having given way to fear.

I admit I don't always have the forces of breakdown beat. I've learned enough along the way to understand what's happening and often avoid the worst. My own incidents of breaking bad were preceded by a cocktail mixed with ingredients like inertia, perceived deficits, sabotage, perfectionism, and pain.

My biggest nemesis has been fear, as I struggle with a terrible fear of letting others down. This specific fear has run my life at times in an unhealthy way. I can handle what pain tosses my way. I can defeat inertia at a single bound, if it means I won't let someone else down.

The paralyzing fear of letting others down is what led me to breaking bad.

On one memorable day—my mind broke. My daughter Emily was about 12 years old, and I was picking her up from school. We were about to leave for a long overdue vacation. During this time, I was travelling and speaking 80 to 90 times a year while running an intense, high-pressure business, raising Emily as a single mom, and taking care of my household. At a traffic light near her school, another driver aggressively cut me off. I lightly honked my horn, we made eye contact, the driver looked directly at me and flipped me off.

I don't know why this triggered me, but I completely blew and proceeded to scream a string of vile obscenities. When my daughter describes that day now, she laughs and describes how I somehow managed to stand up in the car. Sadly, I vividly remember looking in the rear-view mirror to see my sweet daughter's face crumple. Disappointment, shock, and fear were evident as tears streamed down across her red cheeks.

I was horrified. I did not even recognize the woman I saw reflected in her expression. I knew in that moment I had to make a significant change.

I understood instantly I must cut back my travel. I knew this meant I would let some people down. I also knew I had to ensure the right focus at home where I was doing the most important job of my life—raising my daughter. Understand, on some level I knew this already. It was not news to me. I remember the day, the exact moment, my mind broke, and it broke bad. It was a crashing wake-up call.

On another day—my body broke. I found myself in the emergency room. My blood pressure at 190 over 130 felt like my heart was beating out of my chest. I couldn't catch my breath, had pain in my chest, and numbness in my arms. I was sure I was having a heart attack. Thank heavens it was a severe anxiety attack. When the doctor told me I needed a break from work and offered to write a letter to my boss, I laughed. Even in the moment I saw the dark humor. I was the boss.

There were many factors leading up to my health crisis. It became crystal clear in one moment I must make a significant professional change, let some people down, and ultimately leave a company I loved, but was unwilling to die for it. I knew in my guts this was absolutely the right thing to do. I had let myself be pushed to a point of breakdown. My body broke—and it broke bad. Another wake-up call.

One day—my heart broke. I knew Noah, my best friend's son, his whole life. He loved to bowl and fish and never met anyone he didn't like. The biggest wake-up call I ever had happened when Noah took his own life at age 17. He and Emily had grown up together, and he was incredibly loved. But we still lost him.

Death is scary. We don't talk much about it. Death is also how we measure life. Without death, the metrics go to zero because we'd have forever to accomplish things on this earth. Death ensures we have a finite time here.

The absolute worst moment of my life was also the most transformational.

At that point I was in an unhappy and unhealthy personal relationship and it was consuming a lot of me. Losing Noah was what it took for me to decide I would no longer tolerate or be a part of an unhealthy, personal relationship. I would again let someone down; however, life is too damn short. I knew this already. It took a crippling blow and shock to the system to see it. My heart broke—and it broke bad. Another wake-up call.

I am still the tenacious little girl in the red booster seat. Life has taught me. I have learned and changed. I've realized sometimes I need to let go. Sometimes I have to say no. Hardest of all, sometimes I will disappoint others, but only so I can say yes to much better, and to the most significant priorities in my life. I've been able to accomplish important milestones professionally and personally.

I am determined to be present where it matters most. I've worked with Noah's mom to put legislation into play to help youth who've been victimized by abusers. I've been able to be hands on in organizations to help youth who are struggling. I've joined an exciting, growing company that sees and values what I do and places great importance on health and taking care of yourself and your family. In fact, our remarkable CEO heard me mention not having time to do some training runs. In support, he good naturedly (but quite seriously) threatened to shut off my Outlook until I had done so! I've spent much more quality time with my daughter and my extended family, even having annual summer vacations together for the first time—and I've been fully present for important times in their lives.

I learned through these experiences the wake-up calls should have been unnecessary. I should have been able to make the necessary decisions without them. And yet, the very fact of recognizing this pattern in my life and realizing why it happens WAS a wake-up call in and of itself, on a larger level. I still struggle. It is easier because I understand and expect to find a breakthrough on the other side of my fear. On the other side of fear, you too will find your breakthrough.

The answers are quite simple, just not easy. If I can do it, you can do it.

I like simple tasks to keep me on track, as the enemy of execution is complexity. I call my plan for successful breakthrough without breakdown Decide, Operationalize, Take Action (D.O.T.).

DECIDE AND DEFINE

Decide and define with great specificity the goal. Identify what you want to happen—and what is needed to arrive there. Then, write it down. This is critical, and hey, there's even science to back this up. A Harvard Business Study found 3 percent of graduates from their MBA who had their goals written down, ended up earning ten times as much as the other 97 percent put together, just ten years after graduation. Don't become stuck on selecting what kind of leather-bound journal you'll write in, simply decide, define, and do.

OPERATIONALIZE

Chunk up your goal into smaller goals and milestones. Listing it as one big project can be dangerous. As an example, no one simply builds a house. They lay a foundation, pound nails over and over, install plumbing and electrical, bring in insulation, build a roof, and the result is a house. Organize your list into an action plan with dates and deadlines.

Build in accountability by soliciting external support. Share your plan with someone else and ask them to hold you to it. If you've ever heard of the practice of having a personal board of directors, this is where the group can come in very handy.

Make a financial investment. Lock yourself into something—put down a non-refundable deposit for lessons or coaching. Subscribe to a membership or join a class; make sure it's something to help you.

Create the pain. Create a situation to cause you pain if you don't move forward with your plan. The late, great

Ron Quintero once shared with me the story of needing to block time to reinvent his business, but he kept accepting speaking engagements and consulting jobs. One day, he shaved his head. Shaved it bald, knowing he would be too self-conscious to leave the house with a bald head—and literally created his plan. If you don't want to go that extreme, you could schedule a presentation and invite people to it in advance. Another strategy is to use a service like Stickk.com to place a bet—if you don't do what you say you'll do, then the money goes to a non-profit you hate! The idea is to put some skin in the game and create a new consequence if you don't complete the behavior right now.

TAKE ACTION

Sounds simple, right? Sure. It is simple, it's just not always easy. Our brain can process information quickly. It can process a facial expression in milliseconds—which is pretty darn fast. If you have an impulse to take an action you feel uncomfortable doing, your brain can pull the emergency brake in those same milliseconds. Marry your impulse to act with an action within seconds. Sometimes we play games with our intuitive side to move into action. Here are a few tricks I know work.

Physically move, change your position somehow. Your body and brain are tied together, and a simple physical change or motion can often propel you to act. How often do we sit planted in front of our computers, usually not with the best posture, often for hours on end, then wonder why we don't feel energized and inspired to take an action? Literally stand up, do a big stretch, fill up your lungs with air, skip around your living room, give yourself a high five, then take action. Make the call, send the email, grab the workout bag. This will amuse your family to no end AND it works!

Time block. When you are procrastinating on an action, block the time to finish it and do not give up the time for anything. Treat it as seriously as a meeting with a big customer or commitment to a family member. Be your own best friend and honor the time you need to move forward.

I also like the just five-minutes trick. Don't feel like working on the project? Great! Tell yourself you'll work on it for just five minutes, and if you don't feel like doing more, you can stop. You don't feel like working out? Super! Walk for just five minutes, and then go ahead and sit down if you want. Need to read a book which will help you learn a valuable knowledge set? Start to read for just five minutes. How does this work? More times than not, the spark carries you further, and you don't stop after five minutes.

Mel Robbins has a brilliant trick she calls a five-second countdown. You literally count down 5 4 3 2 1 and then move. 5 4 3 2 1 and get out of bed instead of hitting snooze, 5 4 3 2 1 and go grab your running gear, 5 4 3 2 1 and make the phone call you've been putting off.

Most people who are stuck want to change and live a better life; the desire is there, and the answer is known. The roadblock is more often taking the action. It's a conundrum. The simplest step is also the hardest to master. Frankly, I say be thankful. It isn't easy. If it were easy, everyone on the planet would be accomplishing new levels of success and growth and breakthrough all the time, and it would be much harder to compete. I have always raised my daughter Emily to be thankful when we receive bad service, or when someone doesn't return a call or follow up. Be thankful for this because this is how so many people in the world are, and if these actions stay true, it enables you to win.

Here's a challenge for you: did you read something interesting in this book to make you want to take an action? Think of someone in your life who you haven't connected with in a while? Want to simply say thank you via LinkedIn to one of the brilliant ladies who bared their souls here? Do it. Right now. Put down this book and take the action. Time block it, text it, message it, do it.

I bet you'll be shocked by what happens. If you can face the force of inertia and procrastination and take the action, you can do anything.

D.O.T. stands for Define, Operationalize, Take Action. D.O.T. also stands for Do One Thing.

In high school, I had a math teacher, Mr. Bailey. Before a test, he always said, *"If you're stuck on a problem, don't sit there staring at it—put your pencil on the paper and do something. Just start working on it."* Even if you don't know what you are doing, the act of working on a problem will often help the right ideas to start showing up in your head. Action isn't always the result of motivation; sometimes action itself can cause you to feel motivated!

Do one thing, just one, to move you toward your goal.

I had a friend who was in a depressed, dark place. One day, she went to her chiropractor who was also a friend and was describing the dark place she found herself in. She shared her frustration about her career, her relationship, her health, her family—everything. Even her house was undone, she complained, with laundry piling up, mail unopened in stacks, and dirty dishes filling the sink.

Her chiropractor friend said, *"Listen, when you go home today, just do the dishes. Don't worry about anything else, just do the dishes."*

My friend went home and did the dishes, then she realized the rest of the kitchen didn't match the clean sink. She thought, what the heck, it wouldn't take long to clean up the rest of the kitchen. The next day she cleaned up the dining room and cleared her mail off the table. After that, she went through her mail. Sometimes it's just about doing one thing. Suddenly, she was tackling the larger, tougher tasks she'd been avoiding.

If the D.O.T. resonates with you, put a D.O.T. sticker on your phone, your laptop, your mirror. I wear a necklace almost every day which is a simple gold dot on a chain. It reminds me of all the most important things.

We must continually evaluate what we are doing to decide if it's working. When one task or project is on track, choose your next goal and start from the top. If it's not working, take concrete steps to change what you are doing.

Stop asking, *"I'm doing all the right things, why don't I have X?"* The answer is, you aren't doing all the right things to have X. You are doing what you THINK is right, but if you aren't obtaining the outcomes you want, something bolder or different is required.

Can we completely avoid the breakdowns in life? No. We do not always cause them. Breakdowns sometimes happen to us. What we can do is control our response. When a breakdown happens, we start on step one and create a new action plan. I've heard it said, Put Your Plans in Pencil. Plan. Write it down. Take action to implement it and recognize you may have to evaluate and adapt.

We will face adversity. Things will go wrong. The climate may change around us. We won't always get it right. When it happens, we adjust our sails and move on. If I can do this, so can you.

In fact, you've already done this at some level. You acted. You picked up this book, you placed the book in your hands and commenced reading. Here you are. You are already extraordinary.

Once when I was waffling with a decision, letting fate take its course, and likely was headed towards a breakdown, my dad told me, *"Honey, be the captain of your own ship,"* and what he meant was crystal clear.

Don't leave your decisions or actions or attitudes or life rest in the hands of fate–grab hold, decide, and do it.

To you, I wish the same. This life is short and it is beautiful. It is yours. Grab the wheel, take the action, and be the captain of your own ship.

ABOUT THE AUTHOR

Sue Woodard

SUE WOODARD BRINGS 30 years of financial services and mortgage industry experience, strategic vision, and leadership to her role as chief customer officer at Total Expert. Her focus is on helping lenders achieve greater productivity and long-term success. Sue started her career at the ground level, became a top producer, then leveraged her knowledge to become a highly acclaimed industry speaker, subject matter expert, and technology executive.

In addition to having hosted a successful financial radio program and making guest appearances on CNBC, Sue has been awarded numerous industry honors, including the National Mortgage Professional (NMP) Most Powerful Women in Mortgage Banking, the MPA HOT 100 list, the HousingWire Vanguard Award, and the NMP Most Innovative Award. She also serves on the board of HOPE4Youth, a local non-profit working to end youth homelessness.

As a bit of a thrill seeker, she has sky dived over Vegas, fire walked on hot coals, Harleyed down Route 66, ran a Ragnar through the desert and cage dived with great white sharks, but claims nothing is more exciting than parenting her millennial daughter in Minneapolis.

Chapter 4

Journey to 7-Figure Success

Cindy Ertman

*"The big challenge is to become
all that you have the possibility of
becoming. You cannot believe what it
does to the human spirit to maximize
your human potential and stretch
yourself to the limit." ~Jim Rohn*

As I walked onto the stage, I felt a warm rush of blood to my chest. My palms grew sweaty and my heart raced so fast I thought the audience would hear it over my lapel mic. I had managed to walk onto the stage without passing out, so it was a good start. There I was, in front of hundreds of people, who were expecting to be enlightened about the mortgage industry. All I could do was remind myself to breathe and hold on tight to the lectern in case my knees gave out from my shaking.

It was a feeling I had grown to know well. I had after all, agreed to this keynote, despite my crippling fear of public speaking. I always feared the audience could feel my discomfort as I began to speak. The funny thing was, my fear was great, but my passion for serving others was even greater.

I locked eyes with a dear friend and mentor sitting in the front row. When he smiled at me, I felt a wave of calm wash over me. It was then and there, after dozens of fear-ridden experiences on stage and countless hours of conditioning my mind to be present, I instantly shifted focus. Instead of worrying about my performance or what people thought of me, I understood presenting to an audience was not about me. It had nothing to do with me. It was truly all about the people who were in the room; about the people I was there to serve. Since then, I have embodied the belief I am a vehicle to facilitate positive change in the lives of others. In the realization and acknowledgement, I am truly on this planet to serve others, years of struggling to overcome fear of public speaking vanished like a cloud of dust. Looking back, I believe God had a plan for me and helped me realize I had a message to share. When my vision became greater than my fear, my fear took a backseat.

This was the first time I remember truly experiencing the power and profound effects of intention.

As a female in a male-dominated industry, I learned early on being tenacious was an essential quality I needed to keep me in the game. I worked my way up the ranks by sheer merit built on my work ethic, commitment to excellence, discipline, and drive. I was never intimidated by competitors because I knew my fiercest competitor was always myself. With every challenge, I knew failure was not an option for me, so I had to find a way to win!

In the Moment

Growing up with a dad who was mayor of our small town for many of my formative years, I absorbed the knowledge of how to effectively build and nurture relationships. I watched him turn enemies into friends and friends into loyal supporters.

I think what really stuck with me throughout the years was the absolute joy I saw in my father's eyes when he interacted with others. Whether it was the CEO of a major company or the housekeeper who swept the halls, it didn't matter. Dad was always kind, caring, and gracious to everyone. I was often told by friends he made them feel like they were the only person in the room. While the skill can be taught, the sincere, honest interest he took in the person was intuitive. He understood how to be in the moment. It was as natural to him as taking a breath. I strive every day to hold the same presence.

Early in my career, I learned there are key elements contributing to the success of any great leader. I make it my daily mission to incorporate them into my life and my business. I intuitively established systems and processes that brought structure to my day, increased my team's productivity, and helped to carve a path to put my personal mortgage production on the national map. My daily morning ritual consists of dedicated time for meditation, exercise, and education. To this day, this ritual is part of my daily plan.

"When people told me NO on a loan I truly believed in, I knew I had either asked the wrong question or I had asked the wrong person. Know your facts and fight for what you believe in. Be persistent." ~Cindy Ertman

I believe the key to taking my business to the next level came from tapping into the passion I have for helping people, both clients and referral partners. This is a significant part of what I teach today. My desire to help as many people as possible secure their dream of home ownership was the driving force propelling me to be the absolute best I could be every day. I never calculated a commission in my life. I focused on doing the right thing, on helping people make educated financial decisions, and devoted myself to building deep and trusted relationships. At the core, success came from my ability to connect with others in a meaningful way. The lesson my dad taught me early in life has paved the way for opportunities I could have never predicted. I learned to lead from my heart. By diving into my own personal development, I learned to connect more deeply and tap into a deeper part of me to transition from leading my business from my head.

Though I valued and worked diligently on creating systems, tactics, strategies, and processes to streamline my workflow, I came to understand the greatest work I could ever do was the work I did on myself. My focus and awareness has, and always will, serve as the undercurrent in my daily actions to connect with people, be present with them, and listen more intently.

FIND CLARITY

My success in the earlier days did come at a price. It came with late nights and many demands on my time and energy. I have been blessed to raise three beautiful children and I could feel it taking a toll on my family and my marriage.

I remember my first child heading off to the East Coast for college. After he left, I went into his bedroom and sat on his bed and cried. I realized in an instant there were no do-overs. We can't gain even a thread of time back to focus on what matters most.

Fortunately, I had created basic non-negotiables throughout my career including nightly family dinners, showing up to my kids' sporting events, and two-week annual vacations (at minimum) with our kids. I truly did create structures and systems allowing for me to strive towards my greatest goals: to become a strong businesswoman, a great mom, a great wife, and a great friend.

Believe me, I was not always great and I beat myself up when I did not live up to my own expectations of myself. I certainly got off course at times and had to learn to seek help and support to set me back on course.

One thing I know for sure is this life is not a dress rehearsal. We have one shot to do this right and to live our best life.

Creating this structure helped me tremendously to correct my course, as needed, and to stay focused on what mattered most in my life and it still guides me today.

> *"I encourage others to get clear on what's most important. Time goes by quickly. When you get clear on what's most important and create non-negotiables to support your priorities, you create a filter by which all your decisions are made." ~Cindy Ertman*

With one child officially out of the nest and two others right behind him, I embraced a new mindset incorporating a vision of what the next phase of my life would look like. This parental milestone gave me pause and allowed me to scan my achievements so I could identify the goals I had yet to realize. I was suddenly viewing my life with clarity and with a sense of responsibility to my family and to myself. The vision of what I want the rest of my career and life to look like became clearer.

EMBRACE YOUR PASSION

As my business grew and our region expanded and my role changed into leadership management, my passion (over time) began to wane. I had become a talented problem solution specialist and worked closely with our national leadership team. I was great at my job, I was making a great living and began to become increasingly aware I was going through the motions each day, but no longer living the dream. The passion, the fuel that drove me, had escaped. I became fiercely determined to find out WHY and rediscover it!

As I looked at my life, I realized I had climbed to the top of the corporate ladder and had no place to go. I yearned for something more. I had a calling and a mission to help people grow. And while what I did mattered, it was not the same as making a difference in a person's life, building a trusted relationship, and helping them make financial decisions to impact the course of their future.

Then one day a gift arrived on my desk. I had no idea what it was or who it was from. Inside the beautiful box, framed in a deep purple, satin lining, lay a crystal award. I was genuinely surprised to receive this award from *Mortgage Executive Magazine* acknowledging me as one of the Top 100 Most Influential Mortgage Executives in America. Receiving this award was a catalyst for the next shifts in my business, placing my feet on a path down which I have never looked back.

For the past five years, I have received this award. It continues to be a profound honor to be recognized as an influencer. Receiving it triggered a desire in me to use my influence in a greater way. Through meditation and stillness, I realized I had a greater purpose to live.

My passion was to influence the growth of others in a bigger way, and I now have the opportunity to help others acknowledge and tap into their greatest gifts and help them become clear on how to live their best life.

I had always understood and believed in the value of having coaches and mentors in my life. I learned much from the tactical and strategic standpoint of how to be a rock star mortgage loan originator from some of the top mortgage trainers in the business.

When I moved into more of a leadership position in my company, I started working with an executive leadership coach, who helped me focus on developing true leadership skills. He taught me how to think differently, how to communicate differently, and how to embody heart-centered leadership skills. As a leader, I am greatly aware having a strong Emotional Quotient (EQ) is more imperative than having a strong IQ. Again, it comes back to people. It's all about the people, and success starts from the top.

"As a leader, it's our job to create, build, and sustain a great culture and make people know they are valued and appreciated." ~Cindy Ertman

Tragedy is Our Greatest Teacher

"Heart is what separates the good from the great." ~Michael Jordan

I have always felt honored and blessed to have been acknowledged with so many great awards throughout my career. I believe awards are wonderful affirmations of our hard work and effort. Yet for me, true success is about the depth of the relationships I cultivate and the ability to make a defining difference in the lives around me.

In life, we never really know what's around the corner. I was not prepared for the summer of 2004, when tragedy struck and my life was changed instantly.

In one of my relationships I was taught the true meaning of friendship by my friend, Deede Keller. I met Deede when I became the in-house lender of the real estate office where she worked. She was a successful realtor and we had an immediate connection. Eventually, she became my #1 referral partner and a second mom to my kids. She was a beautiful soul sister and my very best friend.

Deede had gone through a difficult divorce. On the surface it appeared to be amicable and her ex-husband stayed close, offering to help her whenever he could. The minute Deede met her new beau, Bobby, things took a sad turn for the worse.

After three days of no return calls from Deede, my worry began to mount. I will never forget the fretful call from Deede's son Michael the Sunday afternoon when he asked,

"Cindy, where is my mom?"

The rest of the story plays out like a scene in a television crime series. The police eventually found my beautiful Deede dead in the trunk of her car.

Sometimes tragedy is our greatest teacher, for it helps us gain clarity about what's most important in our life. Deede taught me two of life's greatest lessons: unconditional love and non-judgement. She taught me some of my greatest lessons and I vowed to continue to share her gifts with the world, even though at the time, I truly had no idea how.

And then I met Jack Canfield.

CHANGE REQUIRES A CATALYST

I remember it was June 2006. I walked into the conference center for Mastermind Summit in Las Vegas. The first keynote was Jack Canfield, known as America's #1 success coach and the co-author of the Chicken Soup for the Soul book series. I was familiar with Jack, but I had never previously met him or heard him speak. I look back on that day and now understand what a catalyst for change the day was in my life, as it became a springboard for a new life to emerge. I had no idea what was on my horizon.

A friend of mine at the conference asked me if I had read Jack Canfield's book, *The Success Principles.* I had not. Shortly after, I purchased his book and read it and studied it from cover to cover. The book sits on my nightstand to this day and is completely highlighted and dog-eared. I felt compelled to learn more from Jack and signed up for his One Day to Greatness seminar in Los Angeles. Shortly after, I made a huge commitment to join his first ever Train the Trainer program. Train the Trainer was a year-long commitment, including three physical weeks together with 100 trainers from around the world. I thought I had signed up for a business training and boy did I get a surprise.

I looked around the room on the first day of our training in San Diego, CA and began to second guess my decision to join the program. This was not what I signed up for at all. I felt incredibly overdressed, as I moved my hair to cover the diamond necklace I had worked hard to acquire and wished I had a pair of flats to change into instead of the high heels I decided to wear. The atmosphere was uncomfortably spiritual. I had completed plenty of self-development work in my life, but I was not expecting this program to be a spiritual dive into the personal development world. I felt exposed and awkward, and for the first time in a long time, I felt like I really didn't belong. I seriously planned my exit strategy for the next three days and thought about how I'd secure my money back.

As much as I wanted to leave and return to my comfort zone, a little voice inside my head said, *"Cindy, just wait, give it a chance,"* after all, quitting has never been my thing. Turns out making the decision to stay in the room, while raising three kids, running a branch, and a top production team, was one of the greatest decisions I have made in my life.

Jack's training was raw and real, and the discomfort I initially felt was just the precipice eventually leading me to my true calling. He taught me how to pay attention to the little voice inside my head wanting to contribute more to the world. I wanted to move to the next level of my evolutionary journey of success and to help others create a defining difference in their own lives. It was time to create my legacy and my company. The Defining Difference was born from a clear vision to make a greater impact. Sometimes, we're ready for a big change and we simply don't know it.

The experience with Train the Trainer helped me paint the picture of a new reality for my life and my business. This new awareness of my greater purpose suddenly flipped a switch in my brain. It immediately opened the realm of possibilities for what the next phase of my life could look like. As the ideas came flooding in, I finally began to feel lighter, like a weight had been lifted. The old future vision I had created for myself didn't have to become my reality.

We all can rewrite a new vision for our future, and it was time for me to birth my new vision for my future. I knew there would be hard work ahead and great uncertainty, but I was committed to create it.

What I have truly learned is highly successful people are willing to be uncomfortable for the sake of growth.

I thrive being outside of my comfort zone today, but it took gaining an understanding of how this propels our life and our business, and it has become the catalyst of my coaching program today. I never imagined making the choice to stay in Jack's Train the Trainer program in 2009 would give me the benefit of Jack's mentorship and guidance, and later, the gift of his friendship.

I've had the great honor to be a member of his international Transformational Leadership Council (TLC) with 150 transformational leaders from around the world for the last five years.

"You are not given a dream unless you have the capacity to fulfill it."
~Jack Canfield

In addition, I have had the privilege to co-author a collaborative book with Jack and be featured in his biographical movie, *Soul of Success: The Jack Canfield Story*.

It sounds cliché because it is true. Sometimes success doesn't come in the exact package you thought it would.

Financial achievement, acclaim, and popular success may feed our ego, but it does not truly feed our soul.

As I held the smooth, sculpted crystal award in my hands the first time I received it in the mail, I made the first of two critical decisions—I decided right then it was time for me to lean into my dream and vision of launching my own coaching and training company, The Defining Difference.

It was time to resign from my corporate leadership role to create the space to live my purpose once again. As I began to share my vision with my business partner of 20 years, a sense of calm washed over me. We both knew this was the right move for me and it had been a long time coming. Risking practically everything I had worked my whole life to attain to go out and start my own coaching business from scratch was the first huge hurdle I had to overcome.

I knew it was time to move from who I had been to who I wanted to become.

The second decision was to leave my disconnected marriage and to do so in a way that left our family unscathed, or as close to it as possible. After 32 years and three beautiful children, there was just nothing left for us to make it work. Ironically, much of the career success I had achieved didn't sit well with my traditional husband.

The bond we shared just seemed to dissolve over time, though we tried for years to recreate it. Neither of us expected our marriage would end, but both of us knew it was time.

This was one of the most personally challenging times in my life. I became relentlessly focused on keeping our family unit intact, despite a challenging divorce. This has since become one of my greatest accomplishments.

Jack taught us E + R = O and I studied this principle: Events + Response = Outcomes.

I held the unwavering vision of the outcome I wanted to create on the other side of divorce and it was my sole focus during the turmoil. My ex-husband and I are good friends today and act as a team in making decisions affecting our children and we sincerely want what's best for each other. By envisioning positive possibilities on the other side of my hurt feelings and broken promises, I was able to navigate the rough waters of divorce and ultimately find calm and peace in the end.

As I continued to let go of things I felt were blocking me from realizing my true potential, I learned the walls confining me were self-constructed. I was confident my new future vision was achievable through deliberate, intentional choices, and remaining true to myself.

I was reminded of something my dear friend and talented mentor, Tim Braheem, said to me, while on the faculty together at Loan Toolbox, *"No one can ever make you great Cindy. You have to want to be great."*

My career success came from a passionate desire to be great and to help as many people as possible secure their dream of homeownership. This passion fueled me to ultimately fund over $2.5 billion in loans with the support of amazing partners and team members.

It was time for me to apply my passion for greatness to a new direction allowing me to live the life I truly desired.

I took back the wheel of my life in 2014 and today I can confidently say I have achieved my true definition of success. I absolutely love my role as a high-performance mortgage coach and I'm inspired by my clients. I'm working smarter, not harder, sharing my gift of helping people tap into their mastery and greatest strengths so they can discover their own defining difference.

"Keep moving towards your dreams and one day you'll find yourself living them." ~Cindy Ertman

---

If I could do it all over again, I wouldn't change a thing. The lessons I learned made me the woman I am today.

One of the greatest lessons I learned was the importance of focusing on what we need to be successful instead of on what's broken.

Many of us live our day-to-day existence on autopilot. Changing our life begins with shifting our choices.

We all possess the ability to rewrite our story and to create our life by design. Sometimes, we just need to consciously shake up our life and take deliberate risks for the sake of our own growth and expansion.

If I had to quantify how I achieved 7-figure mortgage success and beyond, the following key strategies made a huge difference:

- Connection
- Use the power of intentional choice in all areas of my life
- Daily morning success rituals to start my day
- Master my mindset daily
- Do the right thing
- Help people make the right financial decision for them
- Prioritize my day so my business didn't manage me
- Hire the best coaches and mentors
- Help others be successful, not just myself
- Daily gratitude for my many blessings
- Be present
- Learn the importance of working on my business, not just in it
- Surround myself with positive people
- Build deep and trusted relationships
- Listen more and talk less
- Develop a high-impact team committed to excellence
- Let go
- Seek help and support from others when needed
- Master perseverance and never, ever give up
- What I could control and influence (and let go of the rest)
- Daily education to stay relevant
- People first
- Lead from my heart, not from my head

- Share my gifts generously
- Be the defining difference in my own life

Just a few small shifts in our day-to-day choices, mental attitude, and daily routines, can have a profound effect on the way we experience life.

ABOUT THE AUTHOR

Cindy Ertman

CINDY ERTMAN IS the CEO and founder of The Defining Difference® and Mortgage Master Pro®. Her success-based coaching and training companies are devoted to helping people master the power of intentional choice to create a defining difference in their own lives. In *My Journey to 7-Figure Mortgage Success,* Cindy shares the story of how she climbed the ladder of success in a male-dominated industry to become one of the most influential mortgage leaders in the nation. Her life's journey took an unexpected detour, when she discovered the real meaning of success and found her true calling.

Cindy's passion for helping others realize their dream of homeownership laid the foundation for her career trajectory in the mortgage industry. Her incomparable work ethic and talent for building relationships quickly moved Cindy through the ranks, from loan officer to leader, and ultimately helped her build and support the growth of the 12th largest mortgage bank in America.

Leading with the heart of an educator, Cindy shared the strategies and tactics she used to successfully scale her own business with her region's Mortgage Loan Officers (MLO), and also shared her success strategies nationally while she served as a faculty member for the nation's largest mortgage training company, Loan Toolbox, for 17 years.

When she received the award for Top 100 Most Influential Mortgage Executives in America by *Mortgage Executive Magazine*, Cindy realized she was being recognized as a national influencer. The idea she could help others achieve the level of success in business and in life she had achieved was one she could not ignore.

A personal tragedy in Cindy's life led her to participate in the transformative training by Jack Canfield. The experience opened new doors of possibility for Cindy, where passion meets purpose and where she could finally combine the lessons she learned while growing her business to seven figures with her love for helping others.

Soon after, Cindy resigned from all leadership positions and risked what she had spent years building to pursue her calling and dedicate her life to empowering the growth of others.

For the past six years, Cindy has helped high achievers shift the way they see the world and expand their vision of possibility by teaching them her total success approach to business and life.

Cindy's goal is to help her clients gain more out of life by making powerful, intentional choices to propel their income and achieve their peak performance, nurture their health and wellness, build connected referral relationships, and reduce stress by removing the blocks limiting their potential.

Cindy serves as a member of Jack Canfield's esteemed international Transformational Leadership Council (TLC) which was established in 2004 for 150 leaders in the fields of personal and professional development. She's also a founding member of the Association of Transformational Leaders (ATL), a forum for individuals of significant influence in artistic, academic, social, corporate, and humanitarian endeavors.

In 2019, Cindy was featured in the documentary film, *The Evolution of Success*, along with Jack Canfield, Joe Vitale, Natalie Ledwell, and Sonia Ricotti, just to name a few. This documentary series charts the very personal journeys of some of the most successful people in the world focusing not only on their current successes, but also looking back to when their true calling was just an idea or a dream.

Cindy graduated from the University of the Pacific and is a native of Southern California. She enjoys spending time with her three children, close family, and friends and she has a passion for traveling, cooking, photography, entertaining and walking the beach in her local community.

Chapter 5

Defining Moments Create Powerful Opportunities

Ginger Bell

I was seven years old when my brother Gary died. I'll always remember that day. I don't; however, recall my parents telling me there was a chance the heart surgery he was having would lead to his death. I'm sure they knew the risks, and probably, like most parents, only focused on the possibility of the surgery improving his life. Unfortunately, his weak body rejected his new heart and his kidneys and liver quickly failed. He did not make it through the end of the day. That day changed my life forever and made me who I am today. I don't remember saying goodbye to him. I do remember seeing my parents sobbing into dish towels. Embroidered dish towels because my grandmother always had those at her house. To this day, I have no embroidered dish towels in my house. It's funny the things we remember and how it impacts our lives. For me, my brother's death forced me to learn how to figure things out and be a leader. My mother, understandably, could not function after my brother's death. Valium was the drug doctors gave to women during the sixties and my mother found comfort in its numbness. I found comfort in staying busy and getting things done. It was a good combination, I guess, as I had two younger brothers who needed care. It was at this young age I learned how to make lists and delegate. It would be a lesson that served me well through the years and from it I share my first lesson with you.

Successful Leaders Organize, Prioritize, Communicate, Set Expectations, Teach, and Reward

My two younger brothers, Steve and Kevin, were typical boys who were more interested in watching Saturday morning cartoons than they were helping me clean the house. But Saturday morning was the day my mom would go and get her hair done for the week and therefore, our opportunity to clean. The first few weeks I remember telling them to clean their bedroom and bathroom while I ran around doing everything else. An hour later, I would come downstairs to find out nothing had been done other than an argumentative wrestling match over whose tonka truck was whose. I learned I needed to do more than just tell them to do something, and I was not happy about having to clean everything else. I set out to create a list of what chores needed to be completed. This was my first dive into the power of lists and organization still serving me well in my business today. I have a list for everything, and I can help my clients manage large projects through taking big lists and dividing them into smaller lists of tasks needing to be completed. Any project can usually be completed on time with the proper list and deadlines.

With list in hand I trotted downstairs, turned off the TV and stood in front of my brothers. *"I've made a list of what we need to get done today,"* I announced. *"Steve, you're the oldest, so you can pick what you want to do from the list first."* Grumbles ensued, but I stood strong.

"OK", Steve said, *"I'll vacuum."*

Kevin chose dusting and I took on the kitchen. We continued down the list until all the projects had been assigned.

"So, here's the deal," I said. *"The sooner you finish, the sooner the TV goes back on, so if you want to watch TV, get to work."*

More grumbles, but when they saw I was serious they stood up and started to work. This leads me to my next lesson, which is set expectations. As you can imagine, the jobs my brothers did that I had encouraged to quickly finish, were hardly performed with any high degree of standard. I honestly think my brother used his pajama top to trace over the furniture and the floors had maybe three vacuum marks on them. But I had made progress in enlisting their help.

The next week, I showed them how to do their tasks to the standard I had set. Of course, at the age of seven, who knows what that standard was.

In the coming weeks, I learned to turn on music and have them dance crazy dances. I'd offer rewards like pushing them on the swings or playing Legos with them. From my first attempt of just telling them to clean their rooms, I progressed to making a list, organizing, and communicating weekly tasks. I showed them how to do those tasks to the expectation I set, creating fun ways to complete the tasks and finally, rewarding them for a job well done.

When I was together with my brothers after my mother died, it was interesting listening to them talk about Saturday Morning Cleaning at our house. They had fond memories of it and shared they had, like me, taken many of those lessons with them into their careers.

That is what life is about, isn't it? Taking our lessons with us.

As professionals we don't often share our early life lessons with others we know professionally. In fact, we probably have forgotten these early life lessons are still carried with us today. Some good, some not so good.

Life progressed in our family. We all grew up. I moved out, went to school, and got a job. My youngest brother, Kevin, did not adapt as easily to my brother's death, and he resorted to drugs and alcohol at an incredibly young age. By age 15 he had dropped out of school. My parents would keep me up to date on what he was and wasn't up to and I would have talks with him, but he was on a road of his own and we didn't know what to do. I received a phone call from my mother one evening. She was crying and angry and told me my brother had been picked up by the police, again, and was in juvenile detention. She told me she and my dad had made the decision they were done with my brother and were not going to get him, but if I wanted to, I could. This was certainly not something at the age of 23 I had planned on doing, but I was not ready to give up on my brother, so I drove down to Juvie, paid the bail, and picked up my brother. I was living in a large downstairs apartment of a house in Denver at the time. I had a comfortable couch my brother could sleep on. *"Here's the deal,"* I told him, as we drove back to my place. *"Mom and Dad are through with you. You've been screwing around the past several years and it's time to get your shit together. You can stay with me for as long as you want, but here are my rules. First, you're going to get your GED. No questions. We will find out how long it takes, but whatever time it is, you're doing it and you are starting tomorrow. Second, no drugs and I mean none. You are throwing your life away and I know it sucks what we've been through, but what you are doing is not going to get you anywhere. Finally, you will get a job. We will look for one tomorrow."*

And that was it. Which brings me to my next lesson.

SUCCESSFUL LEADERS ARE NOT AFRAID TO BE TOUGH AND PROVIDE SUPPORT

I believe my parents saying, we are done, helped my brother realize it was time for a change. The other part was my ability to be there, be tough, lay down the rules, and provide support. Once I gave him a clear list of what he needed to do and told him I would help him to complete what he needed to do, he did it. He earned his GED and the job he got was with the company that provided concessions to the Denver Broncos. He worked his way up in the company to an executive position and went on to own his own piping distribution company which he sold to another larger company and then became president of the company.

Last year, I was with my brother for his daughter's wedding. At the reception, he stood and toasted me with tears in his eyes and shared he would not be here today, with his family, celebrating this day had it not been for that fateful night so many years ago when I bailed him out and gave him support and direction.

You see, you never know the impact you can have on someone's life, no matter who they are. When you have an opportunity to lead when times are tough and you must tell them something they don't want to hear, can you do it? Will you do it?

I carry with me many lessons I've learned in my life, as do you. It is our responsibility to first, be aware of our lessons and make sure we are applying them, both good and bad. I've learned just as much, if not more from my mistakes, but I've been rewarded most by the lessons I've used to help others and that is life's biggest lesson.

Don't be afraid to be tough.

Don't be afraid to be a leader; we need more of them.

You don't have to be in a management position to be a leader. There are leaders everywhere. Just like the seven-year-old leader who I was forced into becoming so many years ago, I've used those lessons to become who I am today.

If I could talk to that seven year old right now, I'd tell her it's all going to work out and I'm proud of her for all she's accomplished.

I would tell her how brave she was back then and how she helped to frame not only her life, but the lives of her siblings and, in a way, their children as well.

I would tell her that her ability to be a leader with a tough loving spirit helped to frame the life of her son, Blaine, who is successfully working on his master's degree while owning his own esports team. And, most importantly I would tell her she is strong, beautiful, loving, caring, nurturing, and in charge of her life. In fact, she's one heck of a bad ass.

So, how about you? What would you say to the young girl who you once were? Would you tell her everything is going to be ok? Would you tell her how proud you are of her for the choices she made and the accomplishments she has achieved? Would you tell her she was an amazing leader back then and what she did, thought, and became helped to frame who you are today?

I think it's time we let our young version of us know how proud we are of them. It's a great time to embrace who you are, recognize how you got here, and love yourself! I know I certainly do!

Here's to the big you and the little you!

Together YOU are strong!

ABOUT THE AUTHOR

Ginger Bell

GINGER BELL IS the best-selling author of *Success Today*, a book she co-authored with Brian Tracy, *Success Breakthroughs*, which she co-authored with Jack Canfield and her most recent book, *The Edumarketer*, which is a step-by-step guide to using your expertise to educate through videos, webinars, and events. Ginger is also an award-winning producer, speaker, and CEO of *Edumarketing,* a full-service video production and content development agency.

Through the death of her older brother, Ginger learned how to organize, teach, and lead at a very young age. These life lessons taught her you can help people grow in their own lives by developing organized plans and supporting them in the implementation of these plans. Ginger does this in her own business, *Edumarketing,* where she helps organizations and individuals create educational marketing programs and videos.

Ginger's most recent projects include co-producing a documentary on the non-profit organization, *Folds of Honor,* which received two Telly and Emmy Awards and publishing a Mortgage Video Planner to help originators create weekly video content. Her focus on creating educational marketing in the mortgage and real estate industries has helped shape many organizations' educational platforms.

When Ginger is not creating educational content, she is working alongside her son, Blaine, in the esports industry, helping to coach and mentor his professional esports team and raise awareness of this emerging market.

Chapter 6:

The Power of Pennies

Jen Du Plessis

Finally. Home. It only took me 50 minutes. Thank goodness there was no traffic at 11:00 p.m. But was I home? Or was at my hotel home?

My business has grown so much I'm working 14-hour days, and for what?

My body is aching, my mind is fried, I don't have time to have the smallest chat with my kids, the man I'm married to is just a secondary thought, and, hey, did I eat anything today?

How much longer can I run like this? This isn't what life was supposed to be like. Oh well, I need to go to bed so I can start the rat race again tomorrow.

Fifteen years ago, the person described was me. Day in and day out chasing the dream and certainly not living it! I was focused on my business and clients, and it was never enough to be the top producer in my company or have clients and referral partners who loved me. My family loved me (thank God!), but I always put them last. I knew it had to change so I started thinking about where this drive to succeed truly originated.

"We flatter those we scarcely know,
we please the fleeting guests, but
we deal many a thoughtless blow to
those we love the best." ~ Virginia
Krabbenhoft (Jen's Mother)

I come from a large Catholic family and am one of 37 first cousins. Until I was almost 13, I was the only one who was without a sibling. I had 18 aunts and uncles. Two of my uncles were like fathers to me. They took me everywhere with them–cleaning carpets, cleaning offices, cleaning their rental properties, working the family garden center, and even to the oriental trading store. Here is where I learned my work ethic and apparently how to clean!

My parents were hard working, but we were poor, and I mean dirt poor. Dad was a carpenter and functional alcoholic. Mom worked for the family business and was a verbal abuser. My background story is for another time, but the reason I mention it here is to show why I didn't mind spending time with my uncles. It was better than being home with all the yelling, hitting, and throwing.

Most of my childhood memories, aside from the alcohol and abuse, were made with my uncles. They were funny, charming, caring, strict, and always concerned for me. Don't get me wrong, they loved their other nieces and nephews, but they had all moved away and were stretched across the country. These uncles were full of life. A game they played among themselves was to give all the cousins nicknames, such as Dan the Man or Jean the Machine. For me, they chose *Jenny who ain't got a Penny.*

Seriously!?

One of them told me, *"You know Jenny, you're going to be just like your father. You're going to be an alcoholic. You're going to smoke. You're going to have a horrible marriage and most likely you'll be poor too."*

Can you imagine? Of course, I thought it was funny then so I kept a penny in my shoe. Every time they called me *Jenny who ain't got a Penny*, I would grab the penny out of my shoe and say, *"No Uncle, I DO have a penny."*

At first, I didn't understand what he truly meant, but when I did, it made me feel worthless and alone.

This is when I started my quest for a life of proving, which led to proving and perfection. Proving to my uncles, and the rest of the family I would be better and different than my parents. Proving would show everyone I would make something of myself and would make everyone feel proud of my accomplishments. If I were perfect maybe Dad wouldn't drink, and Mom wouldn't cut me down or yell because I didn't clean something right.

Demonstrating the hunger for perfection and acceptance revealed itself in many ways throughout my life. From having stellar grades, becoming a pre-med student, being the best in sports, playing flute and piccolo in the local symphony while I was in high school, becoming an avid speed reader, becoming the only student on the advisory board for the National Lung Association (to learn more about the effects of smoking since Mom and Dad both smoked, and I was experiencing second-hand smoke), being named Miss Colorado Springs, and then runner-up in the Miss Colorado Teen Pageant, being on a competitive rifle drill team, square dance team, soccer player in college, active member of a sorority, becoming a top producer, a national sales manager, and on and on.

I was living a life of proving, until the breaking point 15 years ago.

"One penny may seem to you a very insignificant thing, but it is the small seed from which fortunes spring."
~ Orison Swett Marden

I thought if I was the best in anything or everything I did, people wouldn't judge me, look down on me, second-guess me, or think I was like my parents and amount to nothing. If I could show them I could be much more, life would be great, and I'd finally receive an apology from my uncle.

There was only one (albeit big!) problem to achieving this: *All this hard work for years and years, it turns out, was merely an attempt for me to please everyone else, and not myself.*

"Better to wear out than rust out."
~ John Krabbenhoft (Jen's Father)

Coming to the realization it was time for me to step into my own power was a difficult yet exhilarating time for me. I had to find what was truly important to me, what fulfilled me, and what I wanted. No one else, just me.

The path was tough. I graduated with a degree in Architectural Design and Construction Engineering, so linear, logical, and technical thinking was a part of who I was. After all, being a woman in a male-dominated financial world wasn't easy. Sticking to facts and again proving my worth and value could only come from my results—results as an underwriter, manager, originator, executive, and business owner. Why had I chosen mortgages anyway? Good Lord!

Somehow, someway I needed to dig deeper than I'd ever done before to learn why I acted and performed like I did. That's when I found the true power in my life. You see I was, by nature, a giving and nurturing person. The job, success, and life of proving had made me this way, but it was completely against my core. I was tired of struggling and made the large life decision to change it all. I had to; there was no way I could continue in the same manner.

My family, my husband, and my friends needed me.

I needed me.

Success would have to take a backseat. My production was around $50 million at the time and I would just have to let it go...or so I thought.

If you are casual about your business,
your business will become a casualty.
~ Les Brown

I decided to create an assessment of what I wanted my personal life to look like, then, determine what my real core values were. This approach was the logical side of me tackling the problem regardless of how emotional it might become. Next, I examined how I lived. Was I living these core values or simply talking about living them? For example, if family was a core value, was I placing them first? Had I set up boundaries to ensure they came first? Was I letting external factors (clients, office staff, referral partners, engaging in a life of proving) occupy all my attention?

This wasn't easy. I couldn't turn off the proving and perfection switch. Completing these two simplistic appearing steps took discipline, fervor, and the will to change my life.

I decided to ensure everything I wanted in my life came first. I had concerns and wondered what would happen with the business I worked so hard to build. Nonetheless, I forged ahead. I booked vacations to places I'd never gone, took classes and courses in areas I'd only dreamed of doing one day , planned date nights and being present with my husband, blocked time to read, pray, and be with my children (hoping it wasn't too late). It was imperative these priorities came first.

But how was I going to continue to work if I pursued what was fun and exciting for me? Wouldn't my business fail? And then I'd have to face the music with my uncles. I thought, *"Oh God, please help me push through this!"*

Here is what I realized was coming to fruition–because I was so focused on creating a better life for myself, I naturally began to go to work with more intention and clarity than ever before. In the past, I was a prisoner to my business and everyone in it. Running ragged to complete everything and help everyone. Now, I was clear with who I wanted to help—from referral partners to client types. I narrowed my niches and said goodbye to many complicated relationships. I worked with people who would complement my life.

I was seeing clearly now. Moving from having a mortgage business to a mortgage practice (leveling up my expertise, focus, and intention every day) was going to be key for my success. And it was!

---

*There is no such thing as balance, it's
a total lie! ~ Jen Du Plessis*

To my delight my business didn't decline: instead, my practice grew. It grew in volume (ultimately funding over $1 billion in my career) and team members. Love and patience and being present in all things rather than half witting everything, proved to be the ultimate proving! I was on top of the world; financially (having more pennies), ranking, health, emotion, family, love, fulfillment, joy, time, adventure, culture, and relationships. You name it, I was acquiring it all! I wasn't proving, I was living! Living my legacy while building it.

People talk about work-life balance all the time. For me, it's like eating soup with fork. You are tired, rundown, worn out, living in chaos, lack focus, and more importantly, never truly fulfilled. For instance, let's say you were standing on two boats in the water.

Let's try to maintain balance. You can't because there's too much movement. Neither boat has your full attention. You can't relax and be completely present either. When you finally become too tired, you make a decision to jump to one of the boats (keeping in mind this decision isn't thought through—you're tired and just want it to end– you choose and jump). But are you present on the boat? No. You're exhausted and just want a minute to breathe. Sound familiar? Like the beginning paragraph of this chapter? A balanced scale is 50/50 and never all in.

Work on Purpose to Play with Passion. ~ Jen Du Plessis

What if you could be so clear about your life's desires you go to work with full focus, complete everything in a shorter period of time, work with only the right people, and then leave early to do what you love best? What if you could do this every day? How would your life change?

During the years after making the decision to change how I lived my life, I learned, practiced, and mastered my priorities so I could master my life. It took lots of trial and error but in the end, I was able to narrow everything down to five key strategies allowing me to work on purpose to then go play with passion every day of my life, and attract clients rather than chase them so I wouldn't have to work so many hours. Do these strategies work? You be the judge. In the last eight years of my mortgage career, I worked four days per week, rarely on a weekend, and started three more businesses; all of which I still have today.

These five strategies became prevalent when I was asked by one of my coaches to define what I did to become so successful and still have a commanding personal life. I didn't have any real answers. I first answered, *"Well, I wrote thank you notes."*

She challenged me saying it couldn't be that simple.

So, I said, *"Okay, well, I personally met with each of my clients."*

Her challenges continued. NOW, when I think back on her question, I smile because I did have the answers, I'd just never thought about them deeply enough. I had developed and created a turn-key business that didn't need me to be at the office all day, yet never took a moment to dive into how I was doing everything so well. It became clear there were a few areas where I had become the absolute master: Clarity, Credibility, Community, Communication, and Continuity. Mastering these five strategies made it easy to be successful in business and life.

Focusing in these areas, keeping in alignment with my core values, my life desires, what fulfilled me, who I wanted to work with, and the life I dreamed of having had taken me from $50 million to over $100 million per year in production, and I was working less to live more.

THE POWER OF PENNIES

When I look back to the day so long ago and rewind the comments my uncle said to me; I can't help but think about what my life would have become if my uncle had not said those harsh words to me.

Three years ago, I visited the small town where I grew up. The memories were, and frankly still are difficult to process. Seeing the house where I grew up, every street I passed, parks where I played, and schools I attended; all of this took me back to unbearable times. The truth is, I now know with certainty, I would have a different life had I not been pushed by my uncle.

A quote I found several years ago from Charles Marshbum continues to provide me with solace, "*So, don't pass by that penny when you're feeling blue, it may be a penny from heaven, that an Angel's tossed to you.*" While the naked truth is my uncle's comment cut me to the core, it was also such a blessing to jolt me out of what may have been.

Jenny who ain't got a penny has a lot of pennies today. So there.

One penny has become a powerful symbol. What started as motivation and moved to determination spanned years of desperation leading to inspiration, and finally jubilation.

ABOUT THE AUTHOR

Jen Du Plesiss

JEN IS THE founder of Kinetic Spark Consulting, Black Fox Investments, and Valor Home Solutions. She is the Author of *LAUNCH! How to Take your Business to New Heights*, and her just released book *Business Boosts* where she collaborated with 12 other national speakers. Her next book, *From Success to Significance—Life After*

Breaking through Glass Ceilings, **is** scheduled for release in 2020. She hosts the first mortgage specific and top-rated Podcast, *Stop Talking, Take Action, Get Results!*

She spent over 35 years in residential mortgage lending and was ranked in the Top 1 percent of Loan Originators in the U.S. for many years, as well as being in the Top 200 for four years. She is a self-proclaimed serial entrepreneur with extensive leadership and sales experience.

Today, she is a highly sought-after national and international speaker and coach (traveling with and sharing stages with Tony Robbins, Les Brown, Barbara Corcoran, Darren Hardy, Magic Johnson, and other international personalities), who specializes in creating lifestyle businesses to help solopreneurs, sales professionals, mortgage loan originators and realtors to multiply their results in record time, while maintaining a commanding and prosperous personal lifestyle.

Her mission is to help people identify and then align their core values to enable them to attain more value everywhere in their lives (personal, health, finance, relationships, and business), resulting in the ability to make concise business decisions to create an amazing lifestyle first, and then designing a successful business to fit into their lifestyle.

She has been seen and heard on Good Morning America, Sirius/XM Radio, Voice America, Federal News Radio, and Mortgage News Network. Jen has been featured in such publications as *The Wall Street Journal* and *The Washington Post.* She is a regular contributor for *Mortgage Executive Magazine* and *Mortgage Women Magazine.*

Chapter 7

Ancora Imparo

Kim Hoffman

<u>*Ancora Imparo.*</u>

Still I Am Learning

For most women, our mothers are our first role models for leadership. We grow up watching them navigate their way through highs and lows. My mom wasn't perfect, but she was a fantastic role model. She was stunningly gorgeous, a model in the sixties and seventies, she divorced my father when my two sisters and I were five, six, and eight (I'm the oldest). Mom approached motherhood like a lioness and used every opportunity as a learning moment for us.

Whenever I asked what I should do, she gave guidance and followed with, *"Use your best judgment."* When a challenge presented itself, she'd say, *"Baby, you just got it to do."*

My mom is gone now, and every day I continue to live by the principles she taught me. *Ancora Imparo* is a phrase most often attributed to Michael Angelo. It applies as well to my life.

My career took off shortly out of college when I landed a job in Houston, TX working for the consumer finance division of a Big Three auto manufacturer as team leader. I worked my way through college as a bank teller and then teller manager so getting a job was not hard. I already had experience.

Companies of all sizes were pursuing women in leadership roles (funny, all these years later and we're still pursuing diversity in leadership). Within six months I was nominated to attend the prestigious credit training program. I was excited and my mom was proud. We both knew this could be a game changer for me.

I had to travel out of state to interview. It was my first business trip and I bought a new suit and a new briefcase. It felt like an adventure. I took Mom's advice and dressed for the role I wanted, not the one I had.

I was off to headquarters where I experienced a full day of interviews. They called the process going through the chairs. I called it running a gauntlet.

At the end of the day, I was invited to a group dinner. I was told I would ride with a senior executive. To me, this was perfect. I'd have more time to seal the deal.

Wow was I naïve.

On the ride back to my hotel, the evening took a turn for which I was not prepared.

He began to touch my leg! I froze, but my mind was far from quiet. Suddenly, every hope and dream I ever had about success ran through my mind along with nonstop questions like: How could he know about my traumatic childhood experiences by a *family friend*?

Seal the deal meant one thing to me and another to him.

Did I, in any way, suggest an interest? Was there a way out of this without embarrassing him and destroying my chances for the program? Could I keep my job? So much ran through my head at once, and yet, I never thought for a moment about letting this go further, even if I had to walk back to Houston.

I knew he had daughters based on a picture I had seen on his desk. Gently, but firmly, I moved his hand off my leg and looking him in the eye asked, *"What if this was happening to your daughter?"* Things became frosty, the conversation went quiet, and then he politely excused his behavior.

There were several of these awkward times early in my career. Another time my boss knocked on my hotel door at 10:00 p.m. I didn't answer and was shocked when he questioned me about it the next day! I said I was in the shower, and why would we need to meet so late?

If you engage this behavior even in the least, no good will come from it. Shut it down. I suspect every woman my age has stories to share. For my age group, sexual harassment wasn't taught until five to ten years into my career. I'm gobsmacked when I hear these stories now from young women starting their careers. I recently had to call a friend, a former boss, and tell him it was NOT OK to suggest he spend the night at a young, single female colleague's house. Just the suggestion to her was wrong! Innocent or not, it puts her in an awkward position and, for that matter, him as well! What was he thinking?

I mention this to frame an important fact: you determine the boundaries involving you. Do not let others make you feel pressured to do or act in any way you do not want to act. It is not okay. Have the confidence to say no. How you think about yourself is powerful; your reputation follows you wherever you go so always use your best judgment.

I was admitted to the credit training program and it took me to Florida which was one of 14 physical moves I'd make before finally moving back home to Houston some 30 years later. Before going into the training program, I had never been more than two hours away from a family member. Reality sunk in, as the date of my departure approached. I was about to drive 18 hours to Florida with hopes my life would change forever.

By the time the day arrived, my excitement was gone leaving only sadness and fear. My mother and I cried as I prepared to leave. This was a different kind of crying, it was a, I may never see you again crying. My mom hugged me and whispered, *"Baby, you just got it to do."*

As I write this, I am filled with emotion as tears well in my eyes. I remember saying goodbye like it was yesterday. How proving this event was a pivotal moment in my life. And yet, that day and every fear-laden moment since, has been quietly framed by her words, *"Baby, you just got it to do."*

And so, I did.

BRANCH MANAGEMENT AND A COMEUPPANCE

My first assignment after training was in a small branch. These branches were like smaller companies within the company. As manager, I was responsible for every aspect: profit and loss, growth of the business, people management, origination of every consumer-lending product you could think of, and mixed-use commercial loans.

Managers were also responsible for servicing and loan administration. Being in Florida, my office held a mortgage on a large commercial orange grove, which was in default. The manager before me had started foreclosure proceedings, and I needed to be present for the hearing. My attorney was a pilot and offered to fly us to Tampa. You can almost imagine what a big shot I thought I was. I hated the reason for the trip; there is nothing on the planet worse than this part of our job. No matter what the circumstance, the toll on the family is devastating, and this was my first, and I felt awful.

The outcome of the trial found in our favor and before heading home, our attorney took us to dinner at Burn's Steakhouse in Tampa. This was the first time in my life I experienced a meal as an event. I was introduced to Bananas Foster, still my favorite dessert! From the minute we stepped into the restaurant until we arrived back to the tarmac of Tampa Airport, I kept thinking, wow, look at me, wait until my mom hears about this. Then as I stood waiting to board our plane, reflecting on the day, a much larger private jet pulled alongside our single-engine prop plane. Out walked two striking women, approximately my age, dressed in beautiful designer suits and carrying beautiful briefcases!

My moment was destroyed, like an animated cartoon of a wilting flower. I learned a great lesson, though. There will always be someone with a bigger plane, a more expensive briefcase, and a nicer suit. Stay humble.

My early success presented quick opportunities to move up; I was asked to consider a promotion and move to Memphis, TN. The branch was larger, real estate focused, but failed their annual audit for the second time and needed a new manager. My boss offered me a week to think it over. I smiled and said, *"When do I leave?"* I didn't need to think it over. I realized he thought I was capable, or he wouldn't ask.

I tend to run towards a challenge not from it. It's easy to say no. Growth comes from the yeses. Courage lies in taking on the challenge. I didn't know if I'd be successful, but I did know the experience would have an impact. I knew at the least I would learn from it. If taking on this challenge closed a door, another would open. It is easy to become stuck on the negative what ifs and forget the positive what ifs! In business, we often get do-overs, so take a chance!

BE THE CEO OF YOUR ROLE

We've all had recruiters call us. It's an amazing feeling to realize someone you don't know respects what you have accomplished and what you can do enough to invite you to the table for a career move. When I received my first recruiter call, the only part I remember is being told Fleet Finance is looking to add women leaders to their organization. They have two female executives who are leading the effort, and they would like to talk with you.

I had only worked with men, and for the most part, they had been extraordinarily kind to me. At the time, I wondered why the female aspect was important? The answer became clear as Sharon Moore, EVP and Vicky Thompson, vice president of operations (now the owner of Priority Appraisal Services, one of the first appraisal management companies) came into my life. I will be forever thankful to them. I joined Fleet and managed larger branches. Fleet was more real estate focused, and I transferred when asked. I learned the power and difference between mentors and sponsors through Vicky and Sharon. Until then, no one took a personal interest in my success, but they did! They were willing to bet on me, and I was determined to make them proud.

When someone sponsors you, you're expected to perform so don't let them down. I am still in disbelief and grateful they took an interest in me. They showed me what *Executive Presence* and *Gravitas* were before we used these words! They would walk into a room, and they owned it. It wasn't in an arrogant way, but in a way of confidence, style, and knowledge. I was in awe of this from the beginning. At our annual conference shortly after acquiring another company, Sharon took the stage and said the words I would borrow and use later in my career to align groups, *"Our wagon is going west. We want you on the wagon, but it's going west."* The audience was silent, then thundering applause. We were no longer two organizations, we were one. I will never forget how she commanded the stage and audience. I've yet to see another male or female do a better job.

Vicky taught me to be the CEO of your role. I live this every day, and I've told countless employees, you're the CEO of your chair, your cube, your position! Once I met an employee's mother, and she thanked me for making her son the CEO of his cube. I knew he must have been so proud to tell her this. I almost cried. It takes so little to make a person feel important, significant, and valued. Why leaders don't do this more often is lost on me. Make people feel important; their ongoing efforts will surprise you!

Vicky and Sharon moved on, but their legacy lives in the many women who, early in their careers, were fortunate to learn from them, be inspired by them, and be invested in by them. We are scattered throughout the real estate and real estate finance sector and are paying forward the lessons we learned so well.

It's Not All Roses and Champaign

Although my career continued to progress after Vicky and Sharon left Fleet, it came to a screeching halt when I was passed over for promotion to vice president in favor of a male peer (my friend) who was fresh out of graduate school with hardly any experience. I held the interim role and the business line was growing! I was devastated both because I thought I was the only qualified person for the job (I was) and the person who made the decision was my male boss, who I held in high regard.

Just writing this reminds of how hard I took this. I thought it was the end of my world. I hated the humiliation of hearing colleagues say, *"It should have been you,"* and *"He made a mistake."*

I called my mom crying. I always called her first whether I had good or bad news. This time I think she thought someone died. It was my first career blow—the kind you don't see coming from the person you least expect. I still had a job, a good job, just not the one I wanted.

My mom asked, *"What are you going to do?"*

To which I replied, *"I'll have to stay and do this for a year and then we'll see."*

Can you guess what she said? *"Baby, you just got it to do,"* and she added, *"You can do anything for a year."*

How you handle disappointment will become part of your brand.

She was right. The irony is the boss who didn't promote me left. Later, he called me to join him at his new employer. He flew me to Cincinnati, I met his new team, had a wonderful lunch in the executive dining room, and his compliments flowed. He was pitching me to run warehouse lending for his organization. It was a big job, and I was flattered.

I asked him why I was passed over for the earlier role and he said he didn't have a good answer. It was the worst answer I could imagine. I would have preferred finding out I dropped the ball or my counterpart was smarter. I could accept a reason like that, but his reason was insulting, and begged the question, *"If there was no reason, could it happen again?"*

Despite his attempt at making amends and regardless of the great position and money, I declined the offer.

There's more to your career than position or money. Don't get me wrong, both are important. Who you invest your time with and who you trust your career to are critically important. The people who work for you trust you to do what's right, and you must be a good steward of their careers. Always make sure people can trust you with their careers.

It's Nice to be Wanted

Shortly after this, I received perhaps the best advice of my career! A recruiter called about a position as senior vice president (SVP) of operations and credit for a mortgage company in Philadelphia (as I write this, I am smiling ear to ear). My exact words were, *"I am never moving to Philadelphia."*

I was living in Atlanta and had a great life; if I can't be Houston, then my home is Atlanta. His words changed my life, *"Kim, never turn down a chance to talk to someone who wants to talk to you."* Tony Santilli, president of American Business Financial Services and parent of Upland Mortgage, had seen an article I wrote and wanted to talk to me about the role.

So, still grumbling under my breath I'm never moving to Philadelphia, I flew to Philadelphia for a meeting.

We had a great meeting. I'd never met anyone who could articulate a vision as if it were a symphony. I was captivated by him. He exuded leadership out of every pore. He was elegant and powerful and his vision so explicit you could leave and build the blueprint from memory.

He is awesome. BUT I am not moving to Philadelphia.

I left our meeting thinking this is an excellent opportunity for someone, but I'm not moving to Philadelphia. A few days later, I received an offer and called my mom to tell her I was moving to Philadelphia! A piece of simple advice from a recruiter changed my life. Being willing to take a chance, to take the meeting led to the best ten years of my career and every awesome thing that has happened since.

Working for Tony was an awakening for me! Everything about me changed during my time in Philadelphia. I was challenged in ways I could never dream possible and delivered results I could not imagine. Like Vicky and Sharon, Tony invested in me, but in a way different from Vicky and Sharon's investment. They were structured, traditional, and corporate. Tony was off-the-charts entrepreneurial. Things moved so fast sometimes you did not have time to think before you had to respond. At first, I was out of place. It was beyond anything I was prepared for in my career. Corporations run according to policies and procedures. Entrepreneurs act now and worry later, or at least this one did.

The first six months were like I was in a tornado, and I admit I had no idea what I was doing. A month after I started, I remember being invited to lunch, or so I thought. I walked into our beautiful board room, surrounded by museum-quality art expecting a sandwich and was immediately grilled on our operations by the lead from the investment banking group taking us public. I had not even learned the names of all my staff, had not seen the pitch book, did not know where all the bathrooms were, or even found the best route to and from work.

I was mortified. It is to this day the single most horrific day of my career. I felt like I was on trial and prison looked better than my chair at that moment! This moment could have broken me. My neatly starched shirt was soaked through to my jacket. I was embarrassed, scared, overwhelmed, and shell shocked. As the meeting ended, I remember wondering what the F just happened? How could I have not known the expectations? How come no one told me? And where was that sandwich?

This is when I was told it was a practice session (glad I didn't have a heart attack during practice!) for tomorrow's meeting with the rating agencies for our formal dog and pony (huh?). I'm laughing as I write this remembering, I had to look up what a dog-and-pony show was.

The practice was to show me what tomorrow would be like. The last thing I wanted to hear right then was I had to do this again only this time was for real! A little heads up would have been NICE, and a chance to read the pitch book would have been helpful.

On the way out (with my sandwich), I was finally given the pitchbook. I locked myself in my office, read it cover to cover, made pages of notes only I would know what they meant so no one would notice them, and read every operations report I could find for the past two years. I drove home at 4:00 a.m. and was back at work by 8:00. I watched the clock. It felt like I was counting seconds until I was called upstairs.

As I walked into the same conference room, I did not notice the art or wonder what was for lunch. I was never so laser focused in my life (I did not know I had this much focus). The Moody's team was on one side of the table, and the investment banking group on the other. I was at the head and other teammates were seated at the other end of the table. I felt like this was war and I still needed to recover from the previous day's disaster!

I knew, though, today I would be victorious, or at least I would not embarrass myself again! I slew it, like a professional Ninja. I methodically walked them through operations, loan administration, and, most importantly, underwriting, and credit risk. This was the proudest day of my career and remains a top five!

How in the world could I have the worst day and best day back to back? Preparation! I memorized every number, every trend, knit the conversation to anticipate their questions and answer them before they were asked! It was a mic drop moment if ever there was one. We celebrated later. This meeting made me a player. I knew I was at the table and deserved to be there. Later, Tony gave me a large action figure statue of Lara Croft; it still sits on my desk. You do not know what you're made of until you are called to dig deep. When you do, it changes you forever. I found what I was made of that day!

"Whatever the day throws at me, I'll handle with dignity and grace."

Leaving Tony, I joined a large mortgage company heading up a key platform. I was hired as a vice president and, even though I left a larger title, it was for a bigger job. At the time, I was not hung up on titles if everything else was competitive. I have since changed my belief here. Now I say, *"Don't settle on your title."* It's about more than the company you are working for; it's your standing in the industry, and you've earned it.

When I resigned, my boss asked me why. He said he should have promoted me. I asked why he hadn't. He said I didn't ask! Holy &^%! that's all I had to do! Ask for what you want, don't be embarrassed. Your male counter partners are not embarrassed to ask, and don't make your employees ask to be promoted. We're here to help our employees receive the most out of their careers. If you wait, you'll be asking them during their exit interview what you can do to keep them!

One of my most difficult challenges was working with a female leader. Even today it is hard to believe this happened. I didn't report to her, but she was senior to me and essential in the organization. She was frosty from day one. She was old guard and I was new guard. I had never encountered outward aggression or feeling like this from anyone! I'd ask her if I had done something to offend or hurt her, and she'd dismiss me. She would go out of her way to make things difficult for me. I created a mantra to help me focus and extinguish my emotion over this.

"Whatever the day throws at me, I'll handle it with dignity and grace." I said this countless times a day to counter to what I really wanted to do! She'd try to embarrass me in meetings, talked behind my back, and tried to seek validation for her negativity from others, but my performance and organization relationships thwarted her every effort. I always complimented her and thanked her before correcting her so as not to embarrass her in front

of others. This disruptive relationship existed the entire three years I was there. I never understood why she made this so difficult.

Sometimes we must accept not everyone will like us. It's more important they respect us. In the end, she recommended me for one of the most prominent roles I ever held. I only found out after the fact she had played a pivotal role in me being considered. I sent her a beautiful Tiffany clock and a note thanking her. I am sure if I had let this get under my skin, treated her as she did me, this would have been ugly and forced action by the organization. My message is this: your brand is one of your most valuable assets. Never let anyone move you off center. Whatever the day throws at you, handle it with dignity and grace.

Ladies, a double standard does exist, and I hope I'm not the first to tell you about it! A former boss once told me I was not approachable. I was shocked; literally shocked! I responded by saying I'm sorry (I genuinely was), I certainly thought I was. Could you give me an example? He had only recently joined the company, and I had been there for five years and already had a sense this was going to be one of my more challenging relationships. He says, *"Well, when I came into your office and started talking, you didn't smile."* I'm grateful I didn't say what I thought, which was, *"Really? You show up unannounced, interrupt me, begin speaking while I'm engaged in something, and I didn't smile..."*–you the reader can complete the next two words!

"I'll try to remember to smile" was the real answer I gave him. In the same organization, a male sales leader who

didn't like a credit decision I made came into my office swinging a baseball bat. I knew what he was doing; it was aggressive, unprofessional, and childish.

This same boss glossed over this behavior, saying it was just XXX being XXX.

On another occasion, I picked up a pen that had fallen on the floor and gently tossed it on a table. The same boss told me he heard I had thrown a pen (it was a Cartier rollerball and ladies we don't throw jewelry even if it's a pen). I hadn't but I wanted to at that point. It's hard to work under the scrutiny of the double standard. Don't ever doubt it is real.

Women work hard, often harder than our male counterparts. We must prove more, produce more, and we must do it nicely being sure to smile. What exactly is a resting bitch face, anyway? Is there a resting bastard face?

A male who is direct is seen as a strong leader while a woman is seen as bossy or worse. I watched this my entire career; it hasn't come to be better over the years and, in fact, may be worse.

How many times have you been asked are you in a good mood? Is that question asked of our male counterpart? The fact is sexism does exist. Maybe this is an attribute we can leverage. Instead of fighting it, perhaps embracing it will set us apart as compassionate, nurturing leaders who can also grow the business, manage the profit and loss, and ensure strong careers for our people.

Our teams need different things from women as leaders. Connections at heart may be the difference. I don't mean to knock my awesome male counterparts or employees. We are simply different, and we should exploit the differences for the benefit of our organizations. And remember to smile!

Every experience throughout your career is building one block building upon another along your journey. Eliminate one block and the journey changes. My career has far exceeded my expectations. I'm often in disbelief at the success I have achieved. I never dreamt my life would be so rewarding because people along my journey invested in me, taught me to invest in myself continuously, to embrace the hard, to seek the adventure, and to run towards the challenge. And yes, still, I am learning!

ABOUT THE AUTHOR

Kim Hoffman, CMB, AMP

As chief operations officer for Envoy Mortgage, Kim is responsible for all aspects of loan fulfillment, on and offshore workforces, the customer experience, and service delivery. Kim has more than 25 years' experience in the mortgage industry ranging from servicing, originations, compliance, private banking, operations, process improvement, technology, and service delivery. She has spent the last 20 years having strategic oversight of mortgage operations with prominent industry organizations, including Sutherland Global Services, Morgan Stanley Home Loans, and the Royal Bank of Canada, Upland Mortgage, Fleet Finance, and Chrysler First Financial Services.

She holds a bachelor's degree and post graduate award in operations excellence, process design from Warwick Business School. Kim is a Certified Mortgage Banker (CMB) and Accredited Mortgage Professional (AMP) and was named one of *HousingWire* Magazine's 2016 and 2019 Women of Influence.

She received the Women With Vision Award in 2019, co-sponsored by 20/20 Vision for Success Coaching and *National Mortgage Women's* magazine. Also, in 2019, she was named by the *National Mortgage Professional* magazine as one of the Most Powerful Women in Mortgage Banking.

Kim is an experienced photographer who loves traveling the world in search of great photo opportunities.

Chapter 8

Say Yes Everyday

Laura Brandao

*"You just ruined your life and you will
never amount to anything!"*

These words were said to me when I was 19, unmarried, and pregnant. I thought I was on the perfect path, attending college, and engaged to my high school sweetheart.

In a flash, everything changed. We eloped to Maryland and decided I would stay home with the baby while Tony worked two jobs to support the family. Those couple of years as I left behind my teens are a bit of a blur now, a roller coaster of emotion and change. As we celebrated Jonathan's first birthday, two things became clear to me. First, I had to figure out how to contribute to the family income and second, I had to challenge myself again. Mother and wife are wonderful roles and having experienced both, it was obvious I needed more stimulation.

I asked myself, *what part-time jobs are available at night?*

I had two choices: retail stores or telemarketing. Yep! The winner was telemarketing, and I was introduced to the world of cold calling. The funny thing is I absolutely loved it. I was able to leave the house for some *me time* and take some of the financial burden off Tony.

I quickly became one of the top salespeople because I loved talking to people. However, I was so self-conscious about being a young mom, I lied about my age. I remember celebrating my 30th birthday when I was only 25.

About six months after I started, I put a plan into place for the day Tony and I could buy a house. Earning enough to build a savings account was a challenge.

One day I had the idea of going to see the vice president of the marketing company. Now picture this, I am 21, he is in his mid-fifties, and he does not normally interact with the telemarketing staff. He is old school and only managers can speak to him. Consider my age and the fact I had no experience with corporate America, but it made no sense to me to go through multiple people when I could go straight to the top for an answer. I had the courage of innocence and conviction as I walked to his office before my shift.

He looked up as I knocked on the door and said, *"Who are you?"*

"I'm Laura Brandao, one of the night telemarketers, and I have a question for you."

"OK come in and take a seat."

Years later he told me I was the only person who ever had the courage to go directly to him but hey, what did I know at 21?

I sat and told him my plan to save money to buy a house. I wasn't looking for a raise, I wanted an opportunity to work more hours at night or on the weekend. I made it quite clear I would be happy to help in any way I could.

He asked if I was good at computers.

Well, considering I had only graduated high school two years earlier, I quickly answered, *"Yes!"*

That very night I stayed late running reports. I didn't just run reports, I reviewed them, I analyzed them, and I produced a full sales analysis with production recommendations which I left on every vice president's desk.

Having the courage to walk into the vice president of marketing's office and ask a question launched me into the mortgage industry because I was instantly promoted to the night supervisor of the Champion Mortgage lead generation campaign.

Over the next four years I grew the night crew to over 200 representatives. We became the number one telemarketing company in New Jersey because we had the best lead conversion due to how we trained our team to care about the clients.

This was the first time during my career I consciously engaged in several work habits I still follow today:

Don't be afraid to ask for what you want.

Be undeniable–go above and beyond to the point you cannot be ignored because your results, and your actions, are superior.

Be you–don't emulate or conform to what you think you should be.

Have fun–when you are tasked with keeping 200 telemarketers motivated and engaged, it's important to be creative.

Don't be afraid to talk to others. I have never been afraid to cold call or to network with strangers and this skill has created a large amount of my success.

Take care of your team and you will flourish. We are better together. If you put others first, you will be happy and fulfilled.

After five years having risen to be director of telemarketing, I decided it was time to look for a position where I could give up working on weekends and nights. It made sense to look closer to home, so I applied at a local mortgage broker for a sales manager position. It looked to me to be a perfect fit; I would be responsible for building a team and generating sales via telemarketing.

When I arrived at the interview it occurred to me, I should negotiate better hours. I wanted to work three nights and two days so I could be home with my youngest son part of the time. I pitched it thinking what do I have to lose, right? Guess what? He went for it!

I hit the ground running, placed my first advertisement, and within one week I had 10 telemarketers. Almost overnight, we were generating nearly 100 leads a day which equated to 50 loan applications.

The team was so good it caused pivotal actions to happen. My operations team was overwhelmed, so what does Laura do? I rolled up my sleeves and asked the operations manager to teach me how to process loans. Within a few weeks I mastered Calyx, I processed loans for hundreds of families, and I started the process of setting up warehouse lines so we could become a correspondent lender. Within four months I was promoted to the chief operations officer.

OK, here come two more lessons I learned:

Never let someone devalue you.
Know and Champion Your Value

After two successful years, the mortgage industry entered in to one of those down-turn cycles. The CEO of the company called me into his office to tell me he was cutting my salary by $20,000 because I wasn't worth what he was paying me. Now keep in mind, I had a seven and a three year old at home with a mortgage and my income was higher than Tony. I didn't even hesitate. I resigned on the spot because I knew my worth and my value, and I would never let someone tell me I wasn't worth X.

I left his office and then spent the rest of the day training the team on as much as I could because I will never hurt my team. Fast forward...over the years, all those team members gradually worked for me in different roles. The company I left went out of business.

113

**Be memorable. Every situation
provides you with an opportunity
to be unique and to shine.**

A few months before I resigned, I had been approached
by a recruiter. I went on the interview, but I didn't accept
the offer. However, I declined the offer in a fun way by
going to the card store for a personalized card to which I
added a quote about timing. I sent it to the president of the
company along with a delivery of Hershey Chocolates.

Since I was now unemployed, I called the president of
that company. His exact words were, *"It's my lucky day!"*

I started the job four days after I resigned from the
mortgage broker.

The mortgage industry was exciting in the early
2000s. As we started 2007, the tide quickly turned as we
all watched the implode-o-meter and wondered if our
company would be on the day's list. It was clear to me I
would soon be forced to decide.

On June 9, 2007, decision time came. Even though I
was the director of operations at a wholesale lender, my
future was to either become a government underwriter
or take a leap of faith. My decision came the day I met
Rich, CEO of American Financial Resources (AFR).

My friend (and IndyMac representative) Stacy,
introduced us not long after AFR became a banker. Stacy
told me AFR had an idea to start a wholesale division.
When I heard about this opportunity I said, *"I can do
that."*

Here's the rub: their offer was crazy. No salary. No
benefits. We would offer one product: FHA loans down

to a 500 FICO score. I went to my car and I called my husband. With zero hesitation my husband said, "Laura, you are taking it and I know you will do amazing."

There is a quote by H. Jackson Brown that says, *"Marry the right person. This one decision will determine 90 percent of your happiness or misery."* My husband Tony, the young man I met when I was in high school who worked two jobs to support me and our son, fully understood the importance of me working 60 to 70 hours a week to build a company and bring families home. He continued to help by cooking dinners, doing homework, or just telling me, *"You can do this Laura."*

AFR was a true phoenix rising from the ashes of the financial crisis. Within 12 months we were closing $100 million in FHA loans a month and by 2013 we were the fourth largest FHA lender in the country. In 2009, I became the only woman partner.

Two thousand eighteen was another life-changing year that led to a full transformation. It all started when a conference promoter called and said, *"Hey, I'm planning an event in Irvine, CA in April, and I would like you to moderate the Top Originator panel discussion."*

Sounds simple right? WRONG! Up to this point in my life I was the workhorse and COO who was in the office at 6 a.m., tied to my desk and working 13 to 14 hours a day. In early 2018, margin compression was a real thing and my team needed me to go out and generate business. I stepped out of my comfort zone and said, *"Yes!"* As the weeks passed, anxiety set in causing me to reach out to one of my Account Executives (AE) and asked him if he would moderate the panel and, of course, he liked the idea. Whew. Bullet dodged, I thought. I won't have to be up on stage and everyone will be happy. Or so I thought.

Two days later I took a call from the promoter. *"Hey, I hear you have asked an AE to moderate the panel."*

I said, *"Yep, he will be great."*

"No!" Well, he didn't exactly shout, but he was emphatic about his response. *"I want Laura Brandao; no one else."*

Right there I learned a lesson. As you rise through the ranks there are fewer people who tell you no. When you find those who tell you the truth or challenge you, don't run from them. Keep them close because they are the people who care about you and your growth as a leader.

After the promoter told me I had to do it, I gave it some hard thought. And jumped in with both feet, as always, resolving to be the best moderator I could be. I revised and reinvented myself. I fell in love with learning and teaching myself new skills for this opportunity. I started reading books and watching YouTube videos. I reached out to each panelist to ask if I could spend an hour with them before we went on stage.

On April 11, 2018, I moderated my first event and it was the moment I found my voice. Crazy, isn't it?

I had been in the mortgage industry for 20 years and it took someone telling Laura Brandao no for me to realize I had something to share with others. The event started a ripple that led to awards, magazine articles, video series, live speaking engagements, and podcasts. By October 2018, I was on stage at the Bellagio in front of 2,000 mortgage professionals. This is where an epiphany occurred.

116

Since April 2018 when I first stepped foot on stage, our business had boomed as I was provided with opportunity after opportunity to share my perspective and my voice. When I stopped to think how this happened, I realized it all started when I said YES. An idea burst into my head: what if I did a year of YES where I say yes to everything brought to me? I go into it with no expectations or preconceived notions. I'll be open to the experience and let's see what happens.

Say Yes Everyday has been the rebirth of Laura Brandao. I have lived more in the last two years than the last 15 because every morning I leap out of bed with the challenge fresh in my mind, what do I get to say YES to today?

In October 2018, I was promoted to president at AFR. I was now the face and the voice of the company. Two thousand nineteen brought many more awards and speaking opportunities. In July, I started my daily blog Say Yes. (https://sayyeseveryday.com) Every evening I write what I said yes to during the day. Some days are small wins, and some are monumental. All are special because I will never have those moments in time back, and I said yes to being present and intentional. July 2019 was also the start of the Positively Charged Biz podcast.

Okay, I know you are thinking why in the world do you need another thing to do? Well, remember, I have undergone a transformation and one of the lessons I learned is I love sharing positivity. The idea of creating a show where I can spotlight people who are doing good things in the World and give them a platform to spread joy is irresistible to me.

On July 21, 2019, I interviewed my first guest, Dana Bristol-Smith. She is the founder of Leap to Success, a non-profit helping women who experience domestic violence gain confidence to change their lives. Since 2020, I have interviewed 38 guests, and I have learned something from every one of them. I realized although I am a mortgage executive, I am also relevant outside our industry.

Once again, by saying yes and challenging myself I learned two valuable lessons:

How to listen. Sometimes when you reach the executive level you forget how to listen because you are doing a lot of talking. However, when you are the host it's important to close your mouth, listen carefully, and spotlight your guest.

My guests are all strangers. Ninety-five percent are not in the mortgage industry. When you become an executive, you forget what it's like to not be able to use your name or position to accomplish something. I love challenging myself to research people and call or e-mail them to ask them to be a guest on my podcast.

I have also learned valuable lessons from my podcast guests. I have learned:

We all have pivotal moment(s) in time when it's necessary to choose a path to propel our lives. These are the moments when everything just feels right. When fear of the unknown sets in, follow your intuition.

A strong tribe and community are priceless. You need to find your group; the one where people have your back even in the darkest of days. Once you find it, nurture it. None of us can do it alone. See every person in your life as a puzzle piece. At times you may not realize how they fit into your life, but they will fit at some point if you remain open to the relationship.

Be HUNGRY. Having a burning desire in your belly is more important than intelligence. Everyone has capabilities. Energy is the ember initiating action and change. So feed, but don't appease your hunger.

Gender Physics and imposter syndrome is a real thing. Gender Physics is why we need to be able to balance masculine and feminine energy in our lives because if we sway more one way or the other, we cannot be fulfilled and balanced humans. After one of my female clients told me she suffered from imposter syndrome, I Googled it and found a doctor who wrote a book about it. Dr. Valerie Young taught me 70 percent of all people suffer from feeling like they are not worthy, at some point in their lives.

Until 2018 when I left my office to attend conferences and networking events, I did not realize being a woman executive was special. I was on a mission to see our clients as families, not as loan numbers or dollar volume. I did business family style because it was the right thing to do. Forgetting I am a woman, I made sure my voice, ideas, and movements for change were heard. Most of my philosophies originate from my upbringing:

- Be a good person and do good things and they will come back to you.
- Live each day to the fullest and make a difference along the way.
- When you have an open mind, you are capable of embracing change and life provides opportunities.

119

I am fortunate the mortgage industry found me. The greatest blessings have been all the incredible people I have met along my journey.

Laura 's Lessons

Take care of yourself. This means physically, mentally, and spiritually. As women, we instinctively take care of others, but we need to take the time to feed our minds and bodies with positive energy.

Appreciate your journey. Everything that happens in your life is customized for you. Do not compare your journey to others because we all have our own lessons and roadmaps. Stay focused and enjoy your ride, it is a good one!

Enjoy the moments. We all know how fast time goes especially in the mortgage business where we start at zero every first of the month. Celebrate your wins, big and small, and share them with your home and work family.

You have a lot to learn. If I have learned anything it is I learn something new every single day. Life has many lessons left to teach me and I am looking forward to them all.

Life is exceedingly brief. We may feel like there's all the time in the world, but it passes much faster than you think so tell your family you love them, tell your team you appreciate them, and be grateful for every day.

Remember, success is not the volume of loans or how many team members you have. Success is the joy of having others to share it with while leaving a footprint and legacy for others to build upon.

ABOUT THE AUTHOR

Laura Brandao

LAURA BRANDAO IS the president and the only woman partner of AFR. Armed with a decade of experience, determination, and belief in herself, Laura Brandao started AFR Wholesale in 2007, and she had her high heels in the door and never turned back.

Laura was named one of The 20 Most Successful Businesswomen to Watch in 2020, a Top 10 Most Influential Businesswoman by *Insight Success Magazine*, a 2020 Top in Finance, and was a 2019 NJ Top Women in Business award winner. She has been recognized in *HousingWire's* 2020, 2019 and 2018 Women of Influence editions, named to the 2019 and 2018 *National Mortgage Professional's* Most Powerful Women in Mortgage lists, and was a winner of the 2019 and 2020 Women With Vision Award. In 2020 she became the chair of the AIME Women's Mortgage Network and the chair of the National Association of Minority Mortgage Bankers (NAMMBA) Visionary program.

In April 2018, Laura underwent a transformation when she took the stage for the very first time. As detailed in her story, she realized most of her success, both personally and professionally, was due to a say yes everyday mindset. She continues to enact her theory approaching each day with an open mind and willingness to say YES.

The most significant lesson Laura has learned is to go into every situation with no preconceived notions or expectations. This allows you to do ANYTHING. To experience something new causes no let down because in doing something for the first time we WIN!

Chapter 9

It's All Personal

Maria Vergara

GRACE

I graduated college almost 30 years ago, and I vividly remember graduation day as if only a few years have passed. I'm quickly reminded it was, indeed, a long time ago when my favorite college rock songs were playing on the easy rock channel. As proud as I was of the business degree I earned, I look back and realize there was one lesson the school of business got dead wrong and, in fact, took me years to unlearn. The golden rule, *it's not personal, it's just business* was something I took as gospel. I believe the opposite is true and point to my own career as proof. I attribute my career success as an outcome of several defining moments, each of which were wrapped around personal impact.

I was the youngest child of four. My immigrant parents came to the US in the 1950s and settled in Chicago. My dad worked hard in a factory and my mom stayed home as a young mother learning the ropes of a new country, language, and culture far away from her home base. It was years before they had enough money saved for a down payment on a modest home (and this was at a time when you actually had to save 20 percent of the purchase price). After years of apartment living and hostile landlords who discriminated against our young family, my parents were elated to move into a Chicago bungalow.

Sadly, happy days weren't long lived as gangs began to infest decent, working-class neighborhoods. The Latin Kings were a menacing presence, and they had an eye on my brother. The more my brother outsmarted and avoided them, the more they would harass him.

One hot, summer day, my eldest sister and I made our way to the corner 7-Eleven for some cool drinks and snacks when we were caught in a gang crossfire. I don't recall all the details as I was only 5 years old, but I do remember my sister being brave and quickly and safely taking me to shelter. It didn't take my dad long to borrow money from friends to put a down payment on a house in the suburbs, far away from the city.

The sprawling green lawns and quiet neighborhood seemed like a good place for our family. There certainly was a sense of safety as opposed to the outright danger we had fled. There were also new challenges encountered. The most difficult to overcome was quiet and pervasive. We were the first Mexican family to live in this neighborhood. People were polite, but skeptical. I'm sure the neighbors wondered, *"What are they like? They are a Mexican family from the city. Are these kids in gangs?"*

Our home wasn't big, nor was it the most modern the 1970s could provide. My parents made it the prettiest home on the block. They worked endlessly to tend to our yard, plants, and garden. It was like a microcosm for the Garden of Eden.

We kids didn't have the luxury to hang out with a lot of friends and we didn't have the freedoms the other kids in the neighborhood had due to the watchful and strict rules of our overprotective (justifiably so) parents. Our friends, our social outlet, was us, the family.

I recall my father being adamant we demonstrate to those who were skeptical of us, who we really were, and what we were made of as they say. In time, his strategy worked. Our family made lasting friends in the neighborhood. My parents always presented a graceful attitude; their manner attracted people who were once skeptical about us. Perhaps they came around at first due to curiosity about our culture or my parents' background. Soon curiosity led to support, admiration, and often lasting friendship.

I look back on faded pictures and I understand a magic was happening I didn't see when I was in it. The absolute grace and dignity my parents showed in the face of seemingly insurmountable difficulties, scrutiny, and doubt was a trait I'd tap into time and time again as I grew older.

In business, it is not always about magic. Being successful in business often comes with disappointment, drudgery, and the necessity of performing tasks we simply don't like doing. I firmly believe it is important to show grace and dignity, even if your day starts by mopping up a coffee pot overflow because you happened to be the first person in the office.

I find this to be particularly true at the start of our careers. At times we feel the mere fact we have a degree may be all we need to make it in the door and gain the respect we know we deserve. However, we should remember respect must be earned. We must show we have what it takes to be part of a team, and we are willing to do what others may be too lazy or think they are too good to do. I am not saying be a door mat or give up self-dignity! I am saying, show grace, do the hard stuff, and don't be afraid to earn the respect you know you deserve.

PASSION

My parents were dignified and gracious people whose behavior was determined by culture and instinct. Formally educated they were not. My mom never went past the ninth grade. This was common for girls from small villages in Mexico where work was valued far more than schoolbooks. My father aspired for school and higher education. He had the aptitude, but lack of money and time kept him from his dream of being a mechanical engineer. He gladly settled into a long career as a tool and dye maker.

Together, they raised four kids each of whom pursued higher education. Well, we could attend school if it was

126

close to home. You see, house rules were we did not leave the home unless we were married. Except, of course, if you were the boy of the family the rule didn't apply. (I didn't say my parents were perfect!) We three girls were not pleased with this rule (or others equally as unfair in our view). Surprisingly, neither was my brother. This double standard increased the pressure and expectations on him.

As it turned out, I wasn't the first to go to college. I was the first to break the rule and leave the state for college, though. Oh, the scandal! The disappointment this action caused was palpable for a long time in my family dynamic. I never regretted it, though.

From the moment I set foot on campus at the University of Wisconsin-Madison, I felt like Mary Tyler Moore spinning herself around in Times Square. Too bad I had no beret to throw into the air. My time at the university was exhilarating. I quickly found myself drawn to the school of international business. I loved walking the halls and being able to hear languages spoken from all over the world and meeting kids my age who understood me. For the first time, I felt like I fit in someplace. I wasn't the only one who had parents who didn't speak English well or never ate at McDonald's. I bonded with this new tribe. It felt personal, like home.

I believe the strong love I have for my culture and the fascination of learning from people who were like me and different at the same time drew me into a career in multicultural markets. It's important to identify those moments when you realize what your life's passions are. I first experienced this moment of truth where my career passion and my life's passion entwined seamlessly during my university career. I realized a career in an area I am passionate about would help me to excel. This is what motivates us to continue. What ignites you will not necessarily be the same passion I feel and follow. I encourage you to find your tribe and make sure it feels personal. Detours

By the time I graduated college, pride had overtaken disappointment my parents might have felt over my leaving the family home before marriage. When I look at my graduation picture today, I see a bad hairdo I thought was cute at the time! More importantly, I see my parents beaming with pride. As a mom today, I can appreciate how they felt. For me and my kids, the question isn't college; it's which college. We are fortunate. For my parents who came from poverty, their elation was on an inconceivably high level when all four of their kids graduated college.

The realities of finding a job set in even before I graduated. Because my parents weren't people of deep social networks or financial connections, they couldn't help me with job leads. My siblings chose careers in the medical field and at hospitals. I chose business, a broad and foreign career to the entire family. My dreams of being a foreign diplomat or international buyer were quickly altered by the realities faced by an un-networked, inexperienced young woman. I scoured the newspaper for interviews and anything that seemed like it had a remote chance of growing into my dream job. I was disappointed in the options available and relinquished my dream to choose moving up the ladder beginning as a receptionist at a company with international connections.

Then one April day my father unexpectedly passed away. He was young, only 63 years old, and a few years retired. It was a blow to all of us. He was our rock and compass. Our grief was overshowed by the sobering realization he carried no life insurance. A hard-working man is a virtue but won't leave your wife of nearly 40 years in a good position without other measures in place.

I thought it was surely a mistake. He had worked for one company for over 30 years. How could he retire without any insurance in place? Unfortunately, I came to realize the cost of keeping the insurance after he retired was too much for his budget. He declined the option. Had he started earlier in life, at a younger age, it would have been much less expensive.

This experience altered the course of my professional career. I was thrown into the foreign world of finance and financial literacy. I came out the other side of an intense learning period having made the decision people like my dad need to understand how to protect what they work hard for and learn how to build a brighter future.

Serendipity is a good word. It was at this intersection in my non-career I returned a recruiting call from a large financial institution looking for interns. Even though I was already out of school and had been for a while, I took a shot at it. I studied and passed the qualifications for my series 7, 24, and 6, financial designations understood within the professional community I was entering. I learned quickly, soaking up this new world and speaking a language I never knew existed.

The more I learned, the more I realized this offered a way for me to reach people like my parents. I ventured into the city, the scary place we left long ago, to be a diplomat. I was going to teach them the financial literacy I felt my parents, and everybody, should be taught.

Though I was bilingual, I had to learn how to speak business Spanish. Who knew? I had to learn the language of finance in English, then relearn it in Spanish. After all, how could I explain these literally and figuratively foreign concepts to most small business owners of any nationality? Many of the people I hoped to reach had similar backgrounds as my parents. Distrust of financial institutions and the banking system was one challenge. Their unfamiliarity with basic financial wealth building made my job even more difficult. I did not give up; I put my comprehension of their experience, culture, and language into every connection I made. In time, this bridged the trust gap. With every new client I earned, I felt I was helping my parents. I felt an amazing sense of connection. It was my personal mission.

In a few years, I was named rookie of the year and I fell in love with financial services. I wasn't trying to make anyone a millionaire. I was helping them protect their futures, their hard work, and their legacies. Who knows, I like to think there's at least one person out there who became a millionaire. What's more important is I knew my clients wouldn't have to feel the sting of losing what they worked hard for when life takes an unexpected turn. From that day forward, my whole career has been in financial services and for most of the time I've been serving underrepresented segments.

Don't be discouraged by detours in the road. Paths are rarely linear from point A to point B. Rather career paths tend to look like one of those connect-the-dots pictures we used to do as children. Be patient in your journey. What is it showing or teaching you? Are you paying attention or are you just mad you've been redirected against your will? A wrong turn, whether by your own doing or by the forces of the universe, does not mean a dead end. Be flexible and see where this detour takes you. You may find your tribe and your passion are simply waiting to intersect.

MOVE ON

As several years passed, I went on to different firms and found myself living in a new state as a recently married woman. Over time, I had gradually moved into more mainstream business markets, no longer focused on minority segments. The work was good, but not particularly satisfying. I assumed in time I would find something within the company to match my interests. Much like the days when I was a young, recent college graduate, I was told I would work my way up the ladder. I saw a problem with this theory. In practice, my male counterparts were moving up the ladder much faster than me. Sometimes, my male colleagues with less experience than me would be promoted. This was frustrating to watch and at the time, I believed I had no choice and no say in the process.

I decided to join a local Latino business community. This small group of professionals were like me in many ways. Most came from different parts of the country or world and were seeking common interests in a small city. I thought this would keep me intellectually stimulated

131

until my opportunity came along at work. I also used my career down time wisely and pursued my master's degree.

One day, the company announced it was going to start a multicultural division. I was ecstatic. This was my big break. I could show them the skills I had mastered years ago.

The kickoff meeting was exciting and was almost like how business was portrayed in the movies at the time. We gathered in the beautiful boardroom, catered by the best restaurant in town. Everyone was dressed to the T (this was way before the casual work environment became fashionable). The project offered me good exposure with senior partners, and I was intrigued by the consulting company hired to get this project off the ground. I spent many days and hours sharing my ideas with the consultants, discussing what strategies had worked for me, and which were not worthwhile to pursue.

One day I realized my ideas had made their way into the consultant's fancy PowerPoint presentations, without citing the source. I was furious. I think I was as angry as much for my stolen ideas as I was at the realization of the thousands of dollars invested into the consulting firm simply repackaging my ideas. I attempted to bring my concerns to management, but they weren't interested in listening.

I resigned, without another job in line. I took refuge in the small Latino business group. They encouraged me to take their small organization to the next level and work as their executive director. I worked pro bono and threw myself into this new role. During this time, I met a dynamic businesswoman from Honduras and we decided we could do exactly what the high-priced consulting firm was doing at the company I had just left. We called ourselves Avanza, which means forge ahead in Spanish.

We enjoyed our success in and around our state, helping smaller companies and nonprofits reach underserved markets, especially the Latino market. The work was exciting and made us feel our work was important because people who otherwise wouldn't know about important products or services available to them were being brought to the table because of our connections.

One of the best projects we worked on was with the United Way in helping Latina mothers learn how to build day care businesses. To see women be lifted from welfare to learning how to make a future for themselves was one of the most satisfying experiences I ever had. It was through our small consulting company I became connected to most businesses in town. Word spread about us and our unique skillset. It was through these connections when, after several years (and a baby) later, I decided to go back into corporate. I received an appealing offer to create a multicultural division at a major mortgage bank. With mixed emotions, I took the offer.

I was back on track in my corporate career. I won't ever forget the lessons these years taught me. Think about it. A half step back (resigning without a backup) in the end took me several steps forward, just like the great dance of the tango!

Remember I spoke of knowing when to be humble and graceful to earn the respect? I believe there are times when we must walk away because we know we've earned respect and are not receiving it! There are moments when we need to take a step back, down, or lateral to leapfrog ahead. Don't be discouraged when you hit the glass ceiling. It doesn't mean you can't move up; it means you must move on. Know your worth.

HISTORY IS BEING MADE

After almost a decade in corporate, I felt monotony set in once again. I had come to know an industry group was considered a thought leader around minority markets, the Latinx* segment. I sat on their board and began to really understand the immense opportunities available in this space. I thought progress had been made since I decided to make this a career, but it was apparent the issues were systematic and remained prevalent.

I grew close to the organization's leadership. One day the founder asked me to join him in a new business venture. It would be the first of its kind in the mortgage industry and aimed at helping businesses create strategies to truly moved the needle in dandle rather than the symbolic commitments made by many companies. I spent four years in this role, living the excitement of building a new business and experiencing all the trials and tribulations, as well. I was the marketing department, the business development, the subject matter expert, and the project manager all in one.

It was a few transformative years. During this time, I found myself divorced after fifteen years of marriage and having to start over in my personal life too. I am grateful for having my career to fall back on during these difficult personal times.

For the first time ever, my career became my life raft rather than a compliment to my personal life. I know I would have made it out of the divorce okay, but had it not been for my career, there would have been more collateral damage. I was able to make healthy decisions for me and my kids because I had the financial autonomy to do so.

Apart from a few minor setbacks, I weathered the storm. During this time, I embarked on a project with a large financial institution leading to a job offer tailor made for my expertise and interests. Once again, the experience I had gained in building my own business was just the right training needed for this senior role.

About a year and a half into my new role at this organization, the world literally ceased to exist as we knew it. By March 2020, a rare, once-in-a-century virus, gripped the nation. COVID-19 suddenly took big cities hostage and New York was once again ground zero. Within weeks, states closed and the economy came to a screeching halt. As businesses closed their doors by states orders, the small mom and pops bore the hardest punches.

No one would have thought things could get worse until an unarmed black man's murder at the hands of a policeman was video recorded for all the world to see and George Floyd's name became known around the world. The fury and social unrest following his death has made this man's suffering personal to all of us. Regardless of the point of view or political affiliation, everyone has their own passionate opinion and point of view. It is personal to all of us.

The financial downturn due to the pandemic has only been exacerbated by the social unrest and vice versa. After months of review and study, the scientific data showed people of color were more likely to become ill (non-asymptomatic) and more likely to die of the disease compared to whites. The financial impact and data aren't much better, and the industry has realized it has to do more to break down the barriers to racial inequality and wealth creation.

My background has proved to be a unique skillset now tapped into by my organization. As the date of this writing, I am currently working on several high-profile projects and cross-divisional teams. My personal and professional experience is what qualifies me to be considered an expert in this space. I hope the difficulties our country is facing will result in a transformative era to move us far past partisan lines and towards an honest discourse regarding social injustice and minority homeownership which is a counter stone of wealth building. The mission is personal.

THE LOOK BACK

I am nearly 30 years into this journey, and it's still unfolding. I can see how humility and grace can take us farther than any single piece of paper (aka diploma) ever could. The diploma can get you in the door, but the grace and hard work will keep you around.

Find your passion sooner than later.

Not all of us are lucky to find it early in our careers and if you haven't found it yet, it's okay. Keep looking. If you believe we're put on this earth to make a difference, then you can't give up until you've found your calling. There is no doubt life happens when you're busy making other plans.

The only constant is change and you will be redirected many times. Take these re-routes as an opportunity to see and learn something new. Embrace the twists and bends in the road as they are likely to lead you to a destination better than the one you planned.

Know when you must move on, and recognize when it isn't a move up, per se. Strategic moves backward or lateral can lead to great leaps forward. If it makes you grow, go for it. Your best days are ahead when all these experiences intersect to a point in your personal and professional life and you have the sense of equilibrium.

At no point should your personal life be void of self-actualization nor should your professional life be the only thing satisfying you. Seek a balance, and the balance will occur when you've achieved or have strived for both.

Don't shy away from what makes you feel impassioned, or in creating the career to intertwine with your personal interests. Bring your whole self to work. You are an authentic person. All your experiences have made you who you are.

And remember, in business, it's all personal.

ABOUT THE AUTHOR

Maria Vergara

LUZ MARIA VERGARA (Maria) has led a successful career integrating her love of culture and business. She currently holds a position as director of strategic business relationships at Fannie Mae, a Fortune 500 company.

It's all personal to Maria and for the last 25 years she has intricately woven her bicultural experiences into understanding the needs of the underserved, leading to creative solutions at leading financial services firms.

Maria holds a bachelor's degree in international relations and a master's degree in marketing and has received many industry accolades and recognitions for her expertise in the areas of diversity and inclusion. She is a sought-after speaker and regular contributor to many financial services industry publications. Maria is a native of Chicago and currently resides in Missouri.

Chapter 10

Create a Path and Help
Others Along the Way

Mary Ann McGarry

How can women make their way in a man's world? Every successful woman has faced adversity and setbacks, experienced slights or inappropriate behavior, and found a desired path blocked, delayed, or difficult to navigate. Every successful woman can tell a story about how she made her way forward, despite obstacles, and sometimes because of them. We cannot always control our circumstances. Often, we cannot control how others perceive us, nor what they say or do.

However, we can stay true to our own values, and we can exert a good deal of control even in the most difficult circumstances and make use of everything, including our challenges, to create a positive life for ourselves and for those around us. We always have choices.

In sharing my experience and reflections, I hope I might help one young woman to have a better life, see new possibilities, and be able to make her way in the world on her own terms, and perhaps improve the lives of others, too. Helping others gives life its sparkle.

IT STARTS WITH BELIEF

It's right I should start by remembering my mom's selflessness. She was my rock. My dad was ill for many years. We lost our home and moved to a small apartment, and he died when I was in my early 20s. My mom made it possible for our family to carry on by working five jobs. She showed me the importance of hard work and good values, which she lived all day, every day. She helped me to believe in myself and a future I could create. Born in 1923, she graduated from the UC Santa Barbara, then from the University of Southern California, where she earned a master's degree. She taught fourth grade, including music and gifted programs. In addition to teaching, she worked as a switchboard operator during weeknights and eight hours a day on weekends. She also typed contracts and gave piano lessons, all while taking care of our family.

She said I should get a good education, because *"No one can take that away from you."* She told me I could do anything and having a good education can lead to better options. I believed her. She believed in me. It's essential to have someone who believes in you, and who can help you to believe in yourself.

I knew I wanted a career. I attended Louisville High School, all girls, where leadership positions were, of course, held by the girls. I chose to focus on accounting because I wanted something objective. If I accomplished something, it couldn't be taken away.

From the time I was 15 years old, I didn't receive any financial support from my family. I enjoyed learning and being with my friends in school, and when I went to the University of San Diego, I was part of a study group; learning with others and performing well was fun.

I took jobs as a bookkeeper and as a waitress. In one waitress job, I qualified as a top performer by several objective measures. My supervisor said I was doing great, then propositioned me and made clear my promotion depended on a yes. Instead, I said no, thanks and left the job the next day, communicating to management what had happened.

Nothing came of it, in the sense he stayed on with the company. I learned from the experience. I said earlier you always have choices and can exert some control over your circumstances, and it's true. However, it's rarely simple. A friend who worked at the restaurant was a single mom and depended on her job. She might have made a different choice faced with the same circumstance. It was relatively easy for me to leave and find other work. It's not always easy.

This problem with propositions or inappropriate comments was repeated in other circumstances over the years. Some men let me know I wasn't what they thought I should be. They said I smiled or laughed too much, or I was too cute, or my suits were too bright. The comments affected me. However, I learned to shake them off and use them as fuel to reach my goals. Ultimately, these circumstances reinforced my resolve. Although I couldn't always control what others said, I could control my own response and direct my energies where they would make a difference.

When I was 19 years old, I met Kevin. We married after I graduated from college. He is a natural leader with a good understanding of people. In our early years together, he studied for his doctorate in leadership. He believed in me and was proud of me. When our children arrived (our twin boys Mike and Pat in 1986, Tim in 1990, and Matt in 1996), Kevin shared the work as my partner.

At the time Kevin and I were starting our married life together, I joined Peat Marwick Mitchell in San Diego. I was drawn to the challenge and fast pace. I learned one business with one team, then another business with another team, analyzing problems and making recommendations. It was like working on an advanced degree.

ASK AND THEN DO. RESULTS SPEAK

By 1984, I was recruited to Guild Mortgage by one of the managers at Peat Marwick Mitchell who had left for Guild. I started at Guild in internal audit and was promoted to vice president in my first year. I hired Terry Schmidt, the first person I'd ever hired. She and I became close right away, with a synergy, mutual trust, and respect making both of us more effective, which formed the bedrock for Guild's later success. I recall a time when she and I left a production team meeting, and disgusted, I said to her, *"One day, we're going to run this company."*

I could see we could make Guild much better than it was. I built a team in my first years, with Tee Cherry, Linda Maguire, Mike Rish, and Kathy Wilson, all recommended to me by Kevin, who was coaching football at the University of San Diego.

Martin Gleich started Guild in 1960 and retired, then returned at the start of 1987. The company was losing money and Guild leadership was dysfunctional. He needed to understand what was happening so he could protect his investment. I was on maternity leave for two months at the close of 1986, then on my return, because of my position in internal audit, I reported to him.

Some people told me he was a chauvinist and didn't get along well with women. He said to me, *"Don't tell me you can do something if you can't, and don't tell me you understand something if you don't, and we'll get along fine."* He was well known in San Diego because of his businesses and because he was generous in giving back, although he often gave anonymously. He could be intimidating. He said he'd been told I was really good, then added, *"We'll see."*

I was excited for the opportunity and was always respectful. For 20 years, I always addressed him as Mr. Gleich. He was born in the 1920s and was in his early sixties by 1987. He'd created the company to provide financing for his builder business. In the mid-1980s, all the senior managers at Guild were men, with women present, of course, but in roles of lesser responsibility. I wasn't sure about my future at the company.

Soon, he came to rely on me and my team. He came to me with questions and we would quickly find the answers for him. Once, while he and I were discussing a report on foreclosures, he interrupted and asked, *"What are your goals?"*

His question wasn't related to anything we were discussing, but I was ready. I went into interviewing mode. I said I wanted to be chief financial officer and senior vice president, and if I couldn't do it here, then I'd pursue my goals somewhere else.

He said, *"OK."*

I finished the conversation by saying I could run any department or division in the company. Soon afterward, he promoted me to senior vice president of loan administration. I was 28, with three years of experience at Guild, leading 90 people. Up until then, I'd only managed five.

I said, *"I won't let you down,"* and I didn't. With my team, I re-engineered the loan administration division. It needed a complete re-thinking, to be sure the systems and processes were analyzed and re-organized. This project was the greatest accomplishment of my career. For our team, the work was fun. We loved it. Everyone brought different talents and high energy to projects, often working late and on weekends. I hired football players as temps. They were afraid of not performing well for Kevin. They worked tirelessly and were always positive.

I prioritized and attacked one problem at a time, identifying the root cause and adding controls, working to create a path for people to move up in the company. As I gained experience and moved from one organizational area to another, I prepared someone to assume my responsibilities. Terry became assistant controller, then moved up in finance, and is president today. Tee held many different positions in servicing and in production, perhaps more than anyone at Guild ever has. Over and over, I asked Tee to take on a new challenge, and she would say she couldn't do it because she didn't have prior experience in the organizational area. I knew she could learn anything. I would say, *"It's easy,"* and *it's about learning the process and improving systems.* Tee is now a senior vice president of production and the regional manager of the California and Hawaii regions. Mike Rish moved to secondary marketing and is a senior vice president. Rhona Kaninau started as a temp. I recognized she was strong in execution. I promoted her to lead loan administration. Linda Scott brought analytical skills and created information systems that drove our success. She rose to lead our technology and software development division. Without Linda, Guild wouldn't be what it is, today. She brings quiet strength to every project she touches.

In the 1990s, Steve Hops joined Guild, and rose to lead production and retired early when Barry Horn took over as head of production. Steve recruited Cathy Blocker, who soon led production operations. Cathy brought so many valuable talents to Guild, including her expert judgment. Steve and Cathy were also part of our partner group in our management buyout, which included six women and two men.

As my mom believed in me, I believed in them. This group is the foundation for our success. Almost everyone on this team is still at Guild, more than 30 years later. Tee, Rhona, Mike, Linda Scott, and Terry became owner-managers when we structured a management buyout in 2007. I'll return to that later.

TRUST IN YOURSELF

As I've reflected on my career, recently, I've found *The Confidence Code* by Katty Kay and Claire Shipman to be a useful analysis of women and work. The subtitle is The Science and Art of Self-Assurance–What Women Should Know. Kay and Shipman find women, more than men, hesitate and doubt themselves and their abilities, sometimes missing opportunities. The book's focus on self-confidence is near the heart of my story. My recommendation to women is to ask for advancement and to accept promotions, then figure out what's needed. You can learn on the job. For many women, it's necessary to work, so why not take the better job?

According to *The Confidence Code* and my own experience, women believe, more than men do, they need to be nearly perfect at something before taking on more responsibility. By taking risks and believing in themselves and their abilities, they can achieve much more than they would by playing it safe.

Another challenge women tend to own is how to balance work and family. My sense is women try to do it all, 100 percent. It's impossible to be perfect, or to know everything before you take your next step or leap. For women or men who decide not to work, that's completely acceptable. Choose what you want and pursue it. Do your best.

Although self-confidence is important, my career success is not just about me, nor is it just about self-confidence. Our teams built close bonds. We knew we could count on each other and we could keep learning and adapting, and we could succeed together. That's the real heart of my story.

Today, many people at Guild have been with the company more than 10 years, some more than 20, 30, or even 40 years. People are attracted to Guild and stay, partly because they sense we recognize and value performance.

At Guild, women are well represented at every level. Women sometimes tell me they came to Guild because they believed women would be treated fairly. It wasn't that I was trying to create an environment specifically for women. Rather, many of the best performers around me in the 1980s and 1990s were women. Men and women were part of the team. The focus was on fairness, having clearly defined goals, and working together.

THE LEAN YEARS

After my first few years at Guild, with the formation of our team and the re-engineering of loan administration, the next most significant challenge was our management buyout during the Great Recession of 2007-2008. Mr. Gleich was in his early eighties. He told Terry and me in 2006 he'd decided to retire, it was time to sell, and depending on the buyer, we might or might not have jobs. On learning about his plan, I knew it would have been safer for me to find a position at another company. Instead, I decided I would try to keep everyone together.

149

There were 400 of us at Guild, many close friends, and people I cared deeply about. I knew we'd created something worth preserving, and the combination of our platform and people was valuable.

We didn't lose anyone. Terry and I reached out to Dave Fowler and Paul Connolly with Bank of New York for advice. We'd been working with them for years and had a good relationship built on mutual respect. Dave and Paul helped us see we could structure financing for a management buyout. Mr. Gleich hired Mark Stafford, who helped us draft a Confidential Information Memorandum. Everyone in what became our partner group had worked together for 20 years, and we knew we could achieve our goals. We went into action. We borrowed money, took on significant risk, and committed to working to build the company. I was completely committed. As when I re-engineered the loan administration division, I didn't want to let anyone down.

We received several bids in 2007. We were fortunate Mike McCarthy at McCarthy Capital and his team chose to partner with us. They watched to see how we would perform, then went ahead. Before the management buyout, many of us at Guild already behaved as if we owned the company. We felt the same way afterward. We wanted to provide good stewardship for Guild and for our investment partners.

Since the management buyout, we've been joined by many talented people, and by a number of strong companies with cultures like ours, built on a foundation of good values, and focused on collaboration and solution orientation: Liberty Financial Group, based in Washington

150

State (2008), Comstock Mortgage, California (2014); Northwest Mortgage Group, Oregon (2014); AmeriPro Funding, Texas (2016); Cornerstone Mortgage, Missouri (2018); and VITEK Mortgage, California (2019). Many people have strengthened our company by bringing fresh perspectives. We've recruited and promoted senior managers with substantial experience, including Barry Horn in retail production, James Madsen in loan servicing, and David Battany in capital markets. Amber Elwell is our chief financial officer, and David Neylan is chief operating officer. We're a leading national lender, and as we celebrate our sixteth year in business, we're proud of our customer retention and customer service.

THE PEOPLE WHO MAKE IT WORTHWHILE

I hope by sharing my experience I might be able to help one young woman to see she can succeed. Even in a man's world where she doesn't start by owning or running the business, she can set goals, build strong relationships, and create a positive life for herself and for those around her. The idea of the self-made woman or the self-made man is just a myth. Everyone has help from others and can help others along.

I'd like to thank my husband, who has been my partner for 40 years, and my family. Terry Schmidt and everyone on our team made our success possible. Many people came together in building the company.

I talked with my mom every day until she died at age 95, in 2018. She hoped I would share my story. In developing my career and in helping others, I've tried to follow the path she showed me when I was a girl. This recollection is dedicated to her. She set an example of selfless dedication for me and for my family, and for the many people who knew her. Perhaps after reading or hearing this recollection, one girl or young woman will be able to choose a new direction.

ABOUT THE AUTHOR

Mary Ann McGarry

MARY ANN MCGARRY is the chief executive officer of Guild Mortgage. Under her leadership, Guild has grown from its base in the West to become one of the top lenders in the nation by putting customers first, helping people improve their financial position through homeownership and working to strengthen communities.

Ms. McGarry began her career with Guild in 1984 as a supervisor in internal audit. Within three years, she was promoted to senior vice president of loan administration and information technology and in 1988, was named to Guild's board of directors. She held positions as chief financial officer, chief production operations officer and chief operating officer, before being promoted to president in 2005 and CEO in 2007, when she led a management buyout of the company from its founder. In early 2020, she promoted Terry Schmidt to president while continuing as CEO.

Ms. McGarry has been the driving force in the development and execution of Guild's strategic growth plans and objectives. As a result, the company is now one of the largest independent mortgage lenders in the U.S. with more than 4,000 full-time employees and approximately 200 retail branches in 31 states.

Ms. McGarry and her leadership team have established an entrepreneurial culture that values collaboration, while empowering the company's people to be successful in markets across the country.

She has received multiple awards and accolades for her leadership and Guild is consistently recognized for its positive contributions to the communities it serves, commitment to customer service and collegial workplace culture.

Ms. McGarry was trained as a certified public accountant (CPA) and worked at the public accounting firm Peat, Marwick, Mitchell before joining Guild.

She is a member of the board of directors of the Mortgage Bankers Association and serves on the Fannie Mae advisory board.

Ms. McGarry received a Bachelor of Business Administration in accounting with a minor in computer science from the University of San Diego in 1980.

Chapter 11

Success Formula: Passion, Confidence, and Partnerships

Marcia Griffin

Growing up in New Orleans in the 1950s was joyous. Our middle-class family had many friends and lived a great life, despite the obvious pains of an unjust society. Both of my parents were college graduates, and my father, a native Mississippian who was big on education; he had earned a PhD.

Church every Sunday meant an inspiring word, uplifting music, then home, where my father would lecture my brother and me on what Black people must do to progress in a racially segregated world.

He constantly spoke about how our people had so much strength and potential. He would say, *"We are a resilient group of people.*" According to my father, education was the game changer, the door opener for Black Americans to be recognized, and most importantly to land a good job, "*a good government job*".

The whole idea of entrepreneurship was foreign to most Black families during this time. Even though my grandfather walked 20 miles a week collecting payments on insurance policies for his own company, he never viewed himself as an entrepreneur. He felt blessed to be able to deliver good insurance policies. He saw his work as a better way to send his three children, one of whom was my mother, to a good school and hopefully to college.

In those days, Black families in New Orleans looked up to Mr. Minor as a well-dressed, successful businessman, and church deacon. Grandpa's personal reward was to buy two new suits a year at Rubinstein Brothers. Every time I visited him, he showed me his church suits and confessed his thrill about being called *Mr. Minor* when he entered the store. Having a good image and knowing what customers wanted elevated his success. He was proud of his accomplishments.

The example of service, performance, and value to others set by my parents and grandparents shaped my life and career. Neither encouraged entrepreneurship directly, and yet through their actions and words, they imparted the basic principles I consider a great business leader must have. These include consideration for others and putting forth 150 percent to do something you really love, even though others may see another path for you, like the "*good government job*" my father pushed me toward my whole life.

When I was 10 years old, my family and I moved to Nigeria where my father headed the United States Agency for International Development (USAID), founded by President Kennedy. Yes, this was an unbelievable advancement for my father but *why in the world would anyone want to go so far away to work,"* was what my family said about our leaving New Orleans.

Living in Africa changed my perspective on life for the better. I was an impressionable child, an American living in the African nations of Nigeria, Tanzania, and Uganda, attending British schools. In this global environment the perspectives I would take into adulthood were cultivated as I learned the value of gratitude and the importance of treating disadvantaged people well.

In Africa, most people work hard and have little. My father was there for the dignitaries, the big guys, and most importantly, the little guys. He treated everyone, from the servants to his employees and colleagues, with equal kindness and appreciation for their contribution. He equally recognized the servants, cooks, and drivers, and his high-level racially diverse employee base. Everyone's work was significant. This important trait is one I grew to live by and I've carried and remembered it throughout my life.

One of my life-long goals has been to ensure all people receive the treatment they deserve for the work they do. As I carry on the legacy left by my father, I know how much we benefit from doing right by others, helping others to succeed, and encouraging disadvantaged people to move forward.

THE RACE DIFFERENTIAL

My community in New Orleans was all Black. Although I knew racism existed, I never felt different or ostracized.

These feelings changed when I attended a British school in Africa. Their education was superior to what I received in New Orleans. I was also the only Black kid in many of my classes. The teachers often called on me to read or speak to the class which felt like punishment for not growing up in the same classrooms as my peers.

Though I've never been shy, being academically unprepared while coming from a home valuing education, combined with the full awareness I was the only Black person in the class, made me feel shame, left out, and embarrassed. As the years passed, more Black kids entered my classes and my feelings of shame decreased tremendously. Even so, these early experiences cemented my personal beliefs causing me to work harder, to push others forward, to never put people down, and to do what makes you feel happy.

When I started HomeFree-USA more than 26 years ago, I did so without a true understanding of how powerful and important one's personal beliefs are. Having a passion to help others and the ability to bring people together, along with recognizing partnerships matter, has proven to be the foundation of my success. In fact, at the heart of my journey has been the realization of how an average person, one who was never celebrated for being the best in anything, can make an impact when she puts her mind to something and refuses to take no for an answer.

FIND YOUR GIFTS AND ACCEPT NO EXCUSES

I first discovered my unique talents when I started college at Fisk University in Nashville, Tennessee. One of the first people I met on campus was Judi Sims who is still a good friend. Even though she was new on campus like me, Judi presented herself in such a way I didn't think it was possible for her to be worried or uncertain about anything. She was pretty. She exuded confidence and self-esteem. In contrast, I was nervous, felt fat, and wondered how I would make my way on campus. I have since come to understand what I experienced during my first year of college is common. Many college women, particularly young women who come from a sheltered background, gravitate toward someone perceived as prettier, perfect in size, and more confident than herself.

As we became oriented to campus life, Judi would ask me what to do and where to go. I recall wondering about this. Maybe Judi thinks I know more than I really do. Suddenly, a truth hit me. It's all about the perceptions we have of ourselves and others. Perception is not always truth. Some are true and some not so true. Judi saw a confidence in me I hadn't seen in myself.

For the first time, I paid attention to how I interacted with the world.

As I navigated my freshman year of college, I felt comfortable taking the lead. I felt a part of the HBCU (Historically Black College and University) community. I loved speaking up and being the group connector.

Having friends and family who express their fondness for you, feeling like one belongs in an environment, and sensing a level of trust amongst the people you associate with helps to build confidence in one's self.

I wasn't the best student, but thanks to my gift of gab, my grades were decent enough to satisfy my parents. The classes I excelled in were those in which I dealt with other people such as marketing and finance, which meant money.

My social life was the best part of college. Providentially, it also fed into my growing interest in entrepreneurship. When I somehow found myself selling dorm refrigerators with several friends, I discovered my knack for sales. I was able to effectively communicate the benefits of owning one (or two) refrigerators and made a decent commission. I found sales and marketing to be effortless. I've since learned to recognize the feeling of effortlessness as a sign you're nearing your purpose.

After graduating from Fisk, I moved to Washington, DC to live with relatives as my parents had returned to Africa. My father made it clear he was not paying for graduate school. He encouraged me to find a *"good government job."* He believed I should follow a career path—though fascinating to him—sounded beyond boring and miserable to me.

I was in in my last college semester and had turned down a sales job with Xerox. My next steps, as I marched up to Howard University's Business School to see what connections I could make, were taken purely out of desperation. Thank God for Dr. Abner (and maybe also to my ability to sell). I convinced him he needed me in his upcoming MBA class at Howard University. I don't remember what I said, but I knew this was my only shot and it had to work. Fortunately, it did. I received a full scholarship.

More importantly, I recognized when one puts their mind to something and decides it will be so, the Universe will conspire to bring it forth. Taking action on my own behalf and using my ability to convince Dr. Abner to allow me to continue school instead of working a boring job, showed me what I could accomplish when I focused and refused to take no for an answer.

We must be clear about what we don't want to find out what we do want.

EMBRACING MISTAKES

As women, we often focus far more on our flaws and weaknesses than we should. I am no different. My husband can brush off his failures and keep going whereas, I beat myself up and ruminate over mine for far too long. I was fortunate to have a sense of my strengths and what I liked doing, at a decent age, and I had the foresight to create a career centering on those, and even as I led with these strengths, I gave more power to my flaws and fears than merited. Reading, listening to others whom I admired, and practicing positive affirmations while journaling helped me to overcome my fears.

If I had to do life all over again, I would not spend as much time focusing on my errors. Age and experience have helped me to realize this. Today, I recognize and use my strengths: marketing, sales, and public speaking skills, to help people learn about money, financial stability, leadership, and entrepreneurship.

The Power of Partnership

I had no plans to start a nonprofit to help millions of consumers improve their financial standing.

I clearly see how the repercussions of an unjust society have suppressed the quality of life for millions of African Americans. Realizing there is a racial wealth gap has been all too slow in coming. Efforts to address this void in economic progress continue to be necessary. Recent history is filled with examples.

In the field of mortgage and real estate, it is notable to recognize how Black homeownership rates improved after the 1968 Fair Housing Act was passed. Equally notable is how they then declined dramatically during the housing crisis of the great recession. After decades of observing the pains of both Africans and Black Americans, I launched my vision for improving the homeownership success of people of color by starting HomeFree-USA.

When I started HomeFree-USA, I did so partly because I wanted to change the world. Building on the principles instilled in me by my parents, I wanted to help uplift average people like me to do better financially. I passionately believe information, education, motivation, and connections will change the immediate financial stature and long-term financial picture for under-served people. It is a belief I hold, and it has proven to be true.

To be successful, HomeFree-USA had to show our community how homeownership and wealth building was possible, even when they couldn't visualize it for themselves or had never known anyone else who had achieved such. Even with my skills, there was no way I could do this on my own. Corporate partners who grasped the vision and had the means to support it, became pivotal to our growth and sustainability.

My husband Jim and I approached many banks and mortgage companies. Though Jim had strong relationships with some of these companies through his mortgage servicing business, our goal was to encourage them to invest in HomeFree-USA as a new way to connect with Black Influencers and the Black community in a profitable way, so everybody won.

Not surprisingly, doors closed in our faces. Some powerful mortgage leaders treated us terribly. This taught me valuable lessons. Relationships must be built. It often takes time to convince people to invest in your dream; very few will invest in an unknown entity.

Business partnerships are entirely based on relationships. People support those they like and trust. This is true whether money is on the table or not. Providing value and empowering partnerships by shared benefits is about giving more than you are requesting.

The power of partnerships extends beyond the workplace. Without support, there was no way I could have run a business while raising four children. Between my husband, my parents and in-laws, friends with kids, and our housekeeper Vashti, who went far and beyond what we paid her, neither Jim nor I could fulfill our career dreams without partnership supporting us to raise our children. Each of them helped elevate me, so I could, in turn, help others.

By far, the best partnership I have experienced is with my husband, Jim. *There is a direct correlation between success and happiness. Having a life partner who supports you, encourages you, and is pleasant to be around eschews failure.*

PERSONAL RELATIONSHIPS & PROFESSIONAL SUCCESS

It was by chance how I met Jim Griffin. During my senior year at Fisk, I happened to go to the career placement center to discuss the job I was to take at Xerox. Jim, a recruiter for the University of Pennsylvania Wharton School, happened to be there. A long conversation about life and school, mixed with a lot of laughs, made it easy for us to start a friendship. We loved familiarizing Pat Caviness, the other recruiter from Wharton, with Black culture, Black sayings, and soul food, which he ate and promptly fell right to sleep.

When I met Jim, I wasn't interested in graduate school. After several days of conversations and Pat and Jim pushing Wharton, I decided to cancel Xerox and, if I received a scholarship, go to Wharton and start an exciting new life. That was the plan.

Reality proved to be a little different. Wharton accepted my application, but the scholarship was unavailable. This news is what pushed me into going up to Howard University. Fortunately, my luck held out and my full scholarship at Howard University (with Dr. Abner) set me on my path. Jim and I have been together ever since.

What attracted me to Jim was his down-to-earth, nice-guy demeanor. He still smiles and makes people laugh. Being with a light-hearted person who laughs (and cooks) makes a demanding business life and partnership a lot more palatable. I like him as a friend, a business partner, and a husband.

Because we both shared a desire to help others, make money, be flexible, and chart our own path, we created HomeFree-USA together. Jim affirmed and encouraged my entrepreneurship. This was great. I did not know any Black entrepreneurs, but I had been intrigued by it since my sales days at Fisk. Without exposure and encouragement, I would have been stuck in my curated I can't story. Without Jim's encouragement, I might have easily followed my father's wishes and remained in "*a good government job.*"

There's truly poetic justice in this world. I did work for the government for a few years. It happened just after we had our first child and Jim started his property development business. I quickly learned the government job was nice, but not for me. I could not imagine spending the rest of my life going to work clocking in and out and waiting for assignments in a slow-paced environment. A government job served my father well and does so for thousands of others, but it was not for me. I wanted action, flexibility, and the ability to chart my own course, even without a bi-weekly paycheck. Even when my father cautioned me not to overlook the security of a bi-weekly paycheck, it did not matter. *Charting my own course was heaven sent. I wanted to work for myself.*

When the Problem to be Solved
Presents Itself, Listen and Take Heed

Back in the 1990s, Jim was the owner of the largest and only African-American mortgage servicing company in the country, National Loan Service Center. One of the things that bothered him the most at the time was the high rates of default among homeowners of color.

Around the same time, my marketing company business focused on aligning mortgage lenders with the Black community to increase homeownership. Connecting people and partners to produce a positive outcome is my strength.

Bank of America was my best partner. The executive I worked with subsequently retired. She now heads up a professional and financial development program I launched with Historically Black Colleges and Universities to introduce Black students to the banking, real estate, and mortgage industries.

The biggest marketing challenges at the time, and even today for many people of color, were lack of trust in the system, a lack of targeted information related to them, and a lack of professionals with whom they felt comfortable to ask for advice.

One evening, Jim and I attended a mortgage industry dinner and the conversation turned to the low homeownership rate among African Americans. When it was suggested African Americans were not interested in homeownership, I knew the perceived notion was untrue. There were (and are) plenty of African Americans who want to buy homes.

The issue of denials had a detrimental effect on Black Americans. Education is the key to moving past this and putting more African Americans into their own home.

They are successful homeowners when they are given the financial education, the motivation, the preparation, and the confidence they need to put their finances in order and apply for and be approved for a mortgage.

I saw my path laid out before me after the dinner party. I changed my course of action. I decided I would help as many African Americans become homeowners as possible. The casual dinner discussion extended far beyond the meal for Jim and me. We recognized a need to help people better themselves financially and made a commitment to engage a mix of racially and culturally diverse nonprofits to work together to elevate underserved people. This shared sense of purpose during a casual conversation became the foundation for HomeFree-USA.

When I look back on my career and what has led to my success, most notably a zero percent foreclosure rate among the African Americans we have put into homes with our partners, I realize confidence and partnerships go together. Therefore, it is important to choose a mate, associates, and business partners carefully.

When you surround yourself with
people who believe in you, your
passion becomes your purpose, you
are well prepared, and open to change.
This emboldens you to believe in
yourself and live out your dreams
despite any challenges.

The Power of Passion and Purpose

In a nutshell, passion for me is all about the desire to positively impact people's lives, bringing a lot of value to my partners, being happy, and making things happen. When these actions are in place, I feel the money will come. While I consider passion pivotal in business and in life, that alone is not sustainable. Our success will continue because consideration for the people who work for us, showing appreciation for those who support us, and assuring our service is quality and marketed to the right customers are our top priority.

Just like partnerships, passion and purpose extends far beyond entrepreneurship or even a career. My mother was a housewife with a college education. In her day, the primary jobs for women of color were teachers or domestic workers. When my father was offered the job with USAID, any thoughts of her making her own money were tossed in favor of his career.

My father could not have done his job without her. He was a pure academic who loved nothing more than reading and musing about world economics. My mother handled the soft skills like most women of her time. She built external relationships, entertained his colleagues, remembered birthdays, and moved our household to various countries around the world. Her work also took passion. At 94 years old today, she still feels this was her life's purpose. She was an important part of my father's success.

My work is far from complete. I did not take the *"good government job"* my father recommended but my life turned out just fine. Jim and all four of our children are involved in HomeFree-USA today. We proudly work with 58 culturally and racially diverse nonprofit organizations across the country to improve lives though homeownership. Our big and small mortgage banking partners are excellent and together we are closing the financial wealth gap for people of color. We feel financial education, inclusive marketing, and homeownership are the keys to making all lives matter.

Because of HomeFree-USA, thousands of African Americans who never thought they could own are now successful homeowners, with wealth to pass down to their children. While this may be small for some, for the families we serve, it is a miracle. I am thrilled to have been a part of their success. I am committed to making a difference, to changing lives for the better, and to being an outstanding partner to all.

I am happy to say, my passion has served me well and I want to always be better.

ABOUT THE AUTHOR

Marcia Griffin

MARCIA GRIFFIN IS on a mission to financially strengthen people and elevate homeownership success for people of color across America. As founder and president of HomeFree-USA, Marcia has helped thousands to save, keep, and earn more money through homeownership, which she feels is the key to long-term wealth for all people. HomeFree-USA enjoys a remarkable zero percent foreclosure rate among families that have participated in the organization's pre- and post-purchase program. Serving as a bridge between financial institutions and the community, Marcia addresses the needs of homebuyers and homeowners with targeted education, distinctive marketing strategies, and unique lender products.

A recognized homeownership expert and frequent guest speaker, Marcia is a member of the Freddie Mac Affordable Housing Advisory Committee, the Fannie Mae Affordable Housing Advisory Committee, the Ocwen Financial Community Advisory Council, America's Homeowner Alliance, Wells Fargo Housing Foundation Committee, the Advisory Council of the Federal Home Loan Bank of Atlanta, the Mortgage Bankers Association's Council and the Quicken Advisory Council.

Recently, HomeFree-USA launched the Center for Financial Advancement at Historically Black Colleges and Universities (HBCUs). Our goal is to introduce students to the mortgage industry and advance homeownership as an important goal for parents, faculty, and inner-city residents. Most importantly, HomeFree-USA will expand diversity in mortgage finance and increase homeownership in diverse communities.

Marcia is a tireless advocate for nonprofit leaders and for disadvantaged people everywhere. Under her leadership, HomeFree-USA funds and strengthens the capacity of 53 other nonprofits representing the interests of 4.5 million diverse families across the country.

Chapter 12

Chingona

Patty Arvielo

When I was growing up in Los Angeles, girls weren't encouraged to be a chingona. Quite the opposite, in fact. As a young Hispanic girl, I'd often hear mothers tell their daughters, *"Don't be a chingona."*

What's a chingona? Simply put, it's a badass woman who lives life on her own terms.

As I grew to be a young adult, I recognized a strong expectation in my community defining a woman's role. Traditionally, women were the dutiful wife, the mother, the homemaker. In many ways, our value was determined at birth: we were born to be the guys' wives and the mothers to their children and not much more. Women were judged harshly and looked down upon for wanting a career and a life outside the home.

I knew early on the traditional role was never going to be enough for me. I wanted to be a chingona. I wanted to *own* being a chingona. I wasn't going to live by society's longstanding rules. I was going to make my own way and chart my own path.

To me, the core meaning of chingona is about being a woman who lives her life and is not defined by society's expectations. As a woman, even today, there are social rules laid out for us. The rules are designed to make us feel bad for not conforming. I always resisted the notion to play the game. Even when I was young, I embraced being a chingona. I was in control of my life and did not depend on anyone.

And while following my path has not always led to success, throughout my life I have had more wins than losses.

LEARN AND WIN

Now, let's talk about losses and mistakes. We all make them. It's part of life, but the secret is to never make the same mistake twice. Learn and win! It's a mantra worth chanting. There will always be losses or mistakes. Trust me, there have been plenty in my life. I don't always make the right choices, even now. But I've won way more often than I've lost in my life. And you can do the same!

This learn-and-win philosophy has led me to where I am now; the leader of one of the nation's fastest growing mortgage companies. Being able to help people build a better life for themselves and their families through homeownership is a huge win for me. Homeownership is the number one key to building wealth in our country.

Admittedly, it's not where I thought my career would lead me. Well, that's not entirely true. I really wasn't one of those people who knew at an early age what she wanted to be. For me, it was much more about making as much money as possible. Now, I know this thought may rub some people the wrong way, but I know firsthand what it means to have money and what it means to not have money. And while I didn't grow up in poverty, I saw its raw, painful reality in Mexico. I also saw what it was like to have money in California.

It was immediately clear to me which one of those two ways I wanted to go.

My story is really what the American Dream is all about. I'm the daughter of a Mexican immigrant and a White, Iowa farm boy. I didn't go to college. I've been working since I was old enough and everything I have, I've built myself.

I grew up in South Gate, near Los Angeles. My father was the youngest of 13 kids. His father, my grandfather, was deaf, so my dad was always quiet. As a young man, he left Iowa, moved to California, and went to work at a metal scrapping plant.

My mom grew up in abject poverty in Mexico and moved to California to find a better life.

My parents met through my dad's best friend at the plant. The friend, who is Mexican, was dating a girl, who had a cute friend. Her friend turned out to be my mom and six months later they were married.

Race was never an issue in my house. Being from a biracial family was all I knew, and we never thought anything of it. It was not the way everyone else thought about it. Sadly, I experienced, even as a child, what it means to be a Hispanic in the U.S. and an American in Mexico. I recall my Dad telling a story of what happened not long after they married. It was 1964. My dad went alone to rent their first apartment. On moving day, when he showed up with his pregnant wife, the landlord said, *"Oh, you didn't tell me your wife was Mexican. We can't rent you this apartment."*

Despite being a biracial family, we did not have a close relationship with my dad's family because of the distance between California and Iowa. I think the other reason I grew up heavily influenced by the Hispanic culture was mostly due to having spent much of my childhood in Mexico. My mom was 20 when she had me. On weekends, we went to Tijuana to be with my grandmother. Culturally, my sister, brother, and I grew up playing in the streets of Tijuana. From the time when I could first understand, around four years old, I'd be running around those streets, and people would ask, *"Who do these white kids belong to?"*

That was my identity right there, being a mix of both, Mexican and White.

My Nana in Tijuana really struggled. She was an amazing woman: strong and generous. Something she said to me when I was six years old shaped who I am as a person. I remember what she said word for word, *"You're my grandchild who is going to buy me the house."*

178

She saw in me, before I could, I was going to be a success, and even though I was just six, to this day, it has made a lasting impact on me. I saw poverty and what it looked like. The streets in Mexico where I ran around were dirt. My grandmother's house didn't have an inside bathroom; only an outhouse, and mind you, this was in the 1960s and 1970s, not the 1870s.

Most weekends, this is where we lived, then, I'd come home to our house in the U.S. Truly, there was no comparison. I knew which was better and, more importantly, I knew there could be a life even better than living in our middle-class home. I remember on the drive down to Tijuana my mom would have us kids in the back of the truck. No seatbelts, of course, but we had a blanket. I'd always look up around San Clemente and see these big, fat, white mansions, and I knew it was what I wanted one day!

Anytime I had a little money, I would always save it. My nana called me cheap because I wouldn't lend my money to others. And if someone gave me money, I always hid it and put it away. It wasn't because I was saving for something specific, but instinctively I knew you had to save money to have anything nice in this life. Before I even started working, I was already saving money.

WILL RATHER THAN SKILL

In our family, the focus was on working hard to build a life. I was never proficient in school. Education was not seen as an opportunity. My mom was through with school in the fifth grade, and my dad never went to college. Our family believed it was about will rather than skill. It's something I still believe today. That's not to say education isn't important, but I've found there are plenty of people with a lot of education who don't have the will to do the job.

Having a strong will instilled in me at a young age is a trait I've carried throughout my career. I believe in showing up and working hard. Will is more important than skill. You can teach skill. You can't teach will.

Some would say this is an immigrant perspective. I say it's simply the way I was raised. You work hard, you are rewarded and get what you earned. You don't work hard, you don't get anything.

My first job was when I was 12, helping my mom clean real estate offices at night. I was happy to be doing the work, even if it wasn't exactly glamourous, because I was ready and willing to do the work to climb the ladder. I knew I had to start at the bottom rung and work my way up, step by step, to rise to where I wanted to go.

Plus, I was happy to earn a little money.

A few years later, I landed my first real job. My mom dropped me off at 6 a.m. on Saturday and Sunday at the La Mirada swap meet where I made $25 a day selling wicker products. To me, it didn't matter what it was. I just wanted to make money.

When I was 16, I found the job to set me on the path of my whole life. Thanks to a friend, I was hired by TransUnion Credit as a data input clerk. The pay was $5.50 an hour, which was a lot of money back then. My job was inputting derogatory tradelines. Back then, credit companies kept reports about bank loans including the bank name, how many late accounts they had, and the type of accounts they kept. This information would be organized and go into a big report.

I was not savvy in how the adult world worked. I typed in the data but had no idea why we were collecting information. So, I asked one of the loan officers, *"What are these reports for?"*

"We do home loans."

I was so naïve back then. I asked, *"What do you need a home loan for?"*

When it was explained to me, I asked how much money they made doing what they did. It was more than I was making, so I knew right then I wanted to do what they were doing. I started looking at the Sunday paper every week, trying to find an opening at a loan shop. Eventually, I found a job as a receptionist at a savings and loan where their focus was on mortgage loans.

It was always about climbing the ladder—the trait my Nana recognized in me when I was six—wanting more for myself. I was content to move up one step at a time. The lesson I didn't realize I was learning at the time was how those lower rungs serve us later in life. It does not pay to have it handed to us. The skills, experiences, connections we create, and learn on the lower rungs help us as we climb each step towards success. It's certainly what happened for me.

I climbed step by step, always keeping my eye on the next opportunity.

I looked at each individual task needed to complete a loan for closing. I evaluated each individual job and found out what was being paid. When I was a loan opener, I wanted to be a processor. Then I learned how to be a processor, but I wasn't ready to stop. Back in those days, all processors wanted to be underwriters because back then the underwriter made more.

The funny part is, I lied in the interview and told the hiring manager I knew how to process Federal Housing Administration loans. When I showed up to the job, there was a stack of 50 FHA loans waiting and I didn't have any idea what to do. I was resourceful. (Will rather than skill!) I called a friend in the business, who still works with me today at New American Funding, and she walked me through the process. I learned how to do the job, and I was on to the next opportunity because I wanted to make more money.

To move up the ladder, my next task was to become an underwriter which was harder to accomplish because there wasn't anywhere to learn. Instead, I dug deeper into research and asked people for chances at work to sit next to them when they underwrote a loan. I learned to underwrite. I was 19 years old when I figured out the people making the real money were the loan officers, who were all men. Of course, I did not let this stop me. I saw it as one more challenge to resolve before stepping onto the next rung.

I started cold calling real estate agents to ask for business. The problem? I knew how to do everything on the back end, but I didn't know how to sell a loan. Or for that matter, how to sell myself. For about six months, I had a lot of lunch dates, but no loans. Finally, an older gentleman took a chance on me and gave me a loan denied by another lender.

FAIL EARLY, WIN LATER

Of course, I screwed up my first few loans because I didn't know what I was doing. I learned from those mistakes and never made them again. Even so, I never really did well until I found Countrywide Financial. By the time I was 25, I was running Countrywide's number two branch in the entire country. I was married, with one baby at home and another on the way, and I was killing it at work.

Angelo Mozillo only hired women branch managers and you needed to be an underwriter to be a branch manager. This is where the steps in the earlier part of my career came in handy. I had firsthand experience and knowledge of every piece of the mortgage business. I was tailor fit for what they were doing and it allowed me to flourish there. The whole company was built on women's backs. I naturally gravitated towards that platform, and within a year and a half, the branch was mine.

It wasn't an easy promotion to land because the labeling had started by then. I was called pushy, unmanageable, overly aggressive, demanding, and uncontrollable because I was driven to succeed. Nevertheless, they reluctantly promoted me and gave me a chance. And once I was in the job, I learned a valuable lesson about how to manage people. I was a good producer then, but I wasn't a good manager. I can admit that now.

While I made mistakes as a first-time manager, I learned from the experience. I learned it's important to find people who are great in their respective roles and allow them to excel, and in turn, it allows you to excel, as well.

Learning from the experience wasn't the only mistake I made during that time. Far from it, in fact.

Working with the kind of focus I had at Countrywide cost me my first marriage. I was doing well there, making more money than I ever had. I started thinking I was the be all, end all. Making a lot of money meant I was worth something. I placed most of my focus and energy on winning at work, buying nice cars, and buying bigger houses. I neglected my marriage. I tried to save it. I even quit my job at Countrywide to be a stay-at-home mom. It wasn't for me and it wasn't for us. It was a band-aid placed on a bad wound and it simply wasn't enough to save our marriage.

This was a pricy lesson to learn. It nearly cost me everything. I lost all my money in the divorce. Pretty quickly, I went from being well off to needing to borrow money from my mom. Luckily, I was only 30 years old. Plenty of time to rebuild.

Looking back on it today, I believe there is good to be found here. This experience taught me a valuable lesson I've carried throughout my life: fail early, win later.

I learned what it takes to be successful both in life and in business. I know now I need and want to spend time focusing on both my family and my career, not one or the other. Ironically, as my marriage and career were falling apart, I met Rick, who would become my partner in life and my partner in business.

These days, I wake up every day working on our relationship, and I don't take it for granted. Rick helped me restart my career and eventually became my business partner. He helped me embrace an entrepreneurial spirit and attitude, which didn't come naturally to me. I'd much rather save my money and use someone else's money to build my business. Rick taught me about the risk-reward side of entrepreneurship.

I ended up going to work at a mortgage brokerage called New American Financial. A few years later, Rick, whose background is in marketing, sold his first company and hadn't decided what to do next.

I suggested he come work with me, *"Because mortgage is pretty fun."*

One of his first moves was to come up with a plan to increase our business. He said, *"I will print up some flyers to see if I can help your phones start ringing."*

And did it ever work. Before we knew it, our phones were ringing off the hook. We had two loan officers, me included, and we were up until 2 or 3 a.m. every day answering calls.

It's how we built our business. Rick had the vision and I was the hard worker.

About Luck and Balance

I always thought I was lucky. I believed my success came because I was lucky. After all, I was lucky when I fell into the mortgage industry, right? NAF started to take off when I was around 40 years old. It was then I realized this wasn't happening because of luck. This happened because I am very good at what I do. By then, I'd been in the industry for 24 years; more than most people I was working with had been alive.

It was my commitment to the industry that brought about success. The sense of loyalty I brought into my business, like a typical Latina, was a real strength and a benefit and gave me the opportunity to take the business to a higher level. We'd grown the company into a huge mortgage broker, but we knew it wasn't enough. I remember Rick came to me and said if we really want to build generational wealth for our family, we had to become a mortgage lender ourselves.

We didn't really have any idea how to become a lender, but we embraced the process and the learning aspect and basically taught ourselves how to do it. And while we've been successful in business, I've also worked hard to be successful outside the office.

One thing that drives me crazy is the idea of balance. I speak on panels all the time, and one of the topics always brought up is balance. *"How do you create balance in your life?"* The question drives me crazy. When have you ever heard someone ask a man the same question?

Balance is a symbol of society's pressure to make us feel like we need to conform. Balance is a choice. We cannot BE balanced when career, family and life pull in every direction. We can, however, choose to HAVE balance. I want to empower the younger generation to embrace having both. It is about family and career and recognizing there's a give and take, not an equality between the two. It's not one or the other.

Even with our great success with business, the greatest joy in my life is being a mom to my amazing children, Trevor, Tara, and Dominic. They truly are the light of my life and much of what I do now I do for them. I've found peace with being at home and being a great mother to my children, even though when I'm home I may not be a great leader to everyone at my company.

It's impossible to be perfect while balancing life and work at the same time and I own that. It's about DOING both; not being perfect all the time.

When I'm at work, I'm being a great leader. I'm doing my job for everyone and all the employees. I'm not really being the best mother I can be, and that's OK because one can only do so much.

It really comes down to building systems to work in both places and surrounding yourself with the right people who allow all parts of your life to work as best as they can.

I think society's pressures, the questions being asked of women today, and the narrative we speak to ourselves needs to change. The narrative needs to be around empowering us and having us believe in ourselves, instead of trying to make us look at what we're doing as a choice or a negative trait.

Let's talk about empowering us to be leaders and not about using society's pressure to make us feel like we made the wrong choice.

I don't know men who run around with guilt, but I know plenty of women who do. In my world, Hispanic women and ethnic women especially seem to run around with a lot of guilt. It's because we're shamed culturally for not being at home with the kids. Women are shamed for saying they want to make money or want to be successful.

This is something I battle culturally, and I battle it from society. I'd like to see the narrative change. I think power comes from all the women who are in the workforce today not shaming each other, but building each other up and acknowledging people for making the choices they're making in their lives instead of thinking it should just be one way.

THE IMMIGRANT STORY IS EVERYBODY'S STORY

Another narrative I want to change is to see more competitors who look and sound like me. I want to help lift the younger generation by mentoring them. If you have a C-suite or a boardroom and it doesn't have diverse faces in it, then you're stuck in the past and you're not going to evolve as a company. The views and perspectives contributed from a diverse and inclusive team are priceless.

To make it there, it's important for people to realize no one is going to tap them on the shoulder and offer them more money or a promotion. If you want it, you must go and earn it. Define what success means to you. Then, go to work and make an impact on your goals.

One driving goal for me has always been to take care of my family. My parents are in great health and a few years ago, I was in a position and lucky enough to improve their lives. We bought them a house down the street from us in Newport Beach. Great, right? Yes. Truly. And yet, it also shows us we have not yet reached the top rung when it comes to perceptions. Even though you think you've made it, there are still reminders we have a long way to go.

One day my mother was out walking the dog and struck up a conversation with an older white man who lived in the neighborhood. When she said she lived there too, he was taken aback.

He said, *"Really, where did you come from?"*

"Mexico," my mother replied.

"Oh, well how did you buy in here?" he asked incredulously.

This is just what our life has been like. The perception of Latinos in this country is not what it should be. Latinos come to this country for a better life, just as any human being would. The perception of this man and others is something I work hard to change. I work hard to show people the positive impact Latinos have on this country.

Even so, I struggle with it. I see my mother struggle with being identified and marginalized because of where she comes from or because she speaks with an accent. I often say, *"You know the nanny who's taking care of your kids when you're at work? I'm her daughter. You are here working so your children will grow up to be like me. My mother worked hard cleaning toilets so I wouldn't have to do the same."*

This is the immigrant story. This is my story. I worked hard and still do because I don't want to lose anything. I want to be able to take care of my family. Our core value is family. We do whatever it takes to make sure their life is a little bit better than our life. It's what my mother did. I am her American Dream.

I think this is part of why I've worked so hard. I want to change my family's life for generations to come. I think much of my success has come about because of my attitude and my immigrant perspective.

Remember those labels I mentioned earlier? I was called uncontrollable, pushy, and bossy. Instead of taking the remarks as a negative, I found power and strength in them. I knew I was working toward achieving and climbing to greatness on the next rung up the ladder. Always climbing to the next opportunity. Instead of me allowing unkind labels (heard from mostly males) to beat me down, I used their own words to empower myself, refine my work habits, and ensure I'd be heard.

People often accused me of being an emotional person, but it was never who I was. I was, and still am, very direct. When people are direct, it rubs some people the wrong way. Sometimes it is taken out of context. I've embraced that as my strength. I think part of the reason why my attitude rubbed people the wrong way is because I am a woman. For the longest time, we were boxed out of speaking up and left out of the board room. And we hold ourselves back because we think we need to act a certain way and changing this is the next rung on my ladder. It needs to change, now.

I've embraced becoming a chingona, being a badass. Culturally, I was told my whole life, don't be a chingona. Don't speak up. When I was called a chingona it was not in a nice way. I no longer hear the negativity. Today I embrace it.

I am a chingona.

This is me. This is who I am. This is what I represent. And you're going to hear from me.

ABOUT THE AUTHOR

Patty Arvielo:

PATTY IS AN award-winning entrepreneur and the co-founder and president of New American Funding. A first-generation Latina, she leverages more than 39 years of experience in the mortgage industry to lead the company's sales and operations efforts. In addition, Patty created the company's Latino Focus and New American Dream initiatives to improve the home lending experiences for Latino and Black home buyers. Patty is also a popular keynote speaker for mortgage events across the nation. She is on numerous committees, including for the Mortgage Bankers Association, the National Association of Hispanic Real Estate Professionals (NAHREP), and the Housing Counseling Federal Advisory Committee (HCFAC). She frequently visits Washington, D.C. to lobby for the industry and homeowners. Ernst & Young recognized Patty as 2016 EY Entrepreneur of The Year® Orange County.

Chapter 13

The Night of a Billion Stars –
We Made it Happen!

Regina M. Lowrie, CMB

Traditionally, leadership is thought of as one person standing out front, blazing a trail, charging forward, and leading the way. Women in leadership especially play a critical role in society and for our economy. As author Diane Mariechild said, "*A woman is the full circle; within her is the power to create, nurture, and transform.*"

> *A leader's core responsibilities are to provide vision and direction, inspire a given team to bring their A Game, and remove the boulders blocking*

the way. Leaders do all these things. Extraordinary leaders will tell you they did not, and could not, do all of them alone.

Laying the Foundation

Networking

From the beginning, collaboration was crucial. Building a network of support and contacts outside of your organization is important. I would say this was the single most important factor over the years leading to my success. My parents were my biggest cheerleaders, but I also had two strong mentors who trusted and believed in me. One, a no-holds-barred critic, helped launch my entrepreneurial career. The other, incredibly open about his experiences in business, acted as a sounding board throughout the years. Without their unconditional support, I might not have been able to achieve what has turned out to be several noteworthy accomplishments which have allowed me to surpass my expectations.

Building a network outside of my comfort zone played a huge part in my success. Network! Get involved with any kind of group: professional association, group at work, neighborhood association, local politics, your local hospital, any charity, or any arts organization.

- Pay it forward
- Find ways to help–in all areas of your life
- Find your passion outside of work, too
- Sign up for committees

194

- Take the initiative
- Tell people what YOU think.
- Listen.
- Give and Receive. Whether it is within your industry or meeting once a month over dinner or drinks, group dynamics, even the traditional one-on-one, mentoring and collaboration is important even if it's with your competitors. I had a friend, Nora, who was a senior executive at a competing firm. We regularly exchanged ideas and supported each other. We encouraged each other and learned from each other. I firmly believe in seeing my competition as an ally and a resource.

Early in my career I made the decision to become involved with the Pennsylvania Mortgage Bankers Association, the trade association representing the mortgage industry. Before long, I was nominated to the board of governors. Soon after, I was asked to chair the education committee where I developed a School of Mortgage Banking, eventually accredited by the Mortgage Bankers Association for Certified Mortgage Banker credits. This was around 1987. My network of contacts began to grow and soon my accomplishments were being recognized by the National Mortgage Bankers Association. I continued to serve on the local trade association board, eventually being nominated in 1995, as the first woman president in the organization's 56-year history.

Being the Captain of My Life's Ship

As my network of contacts expanded, so did my career. In 1993, I decided to put a business plan together to start my own mortgage company. I realized I had gone as far as possible using my talents for others. I had built the mortgage operation for this small savings and loan company to over $1 billion. Yet, I rarely had big picture decision-making executive leadership opportunities. In 1993, I made the decision to use my talents for me. I wanted to be in control of my own destiny and create wealth for my family and myself. I decided to pursue personal satisfaction and use my experience and expertise to build an independent mortgage banking company from the ground up.

One of my fellow board of directors' members at the Pennsylvania Mortgage Bankers Association approached me about my business plan. He had heard I was looking to start a mortgage company and I was looking to raise capital. He offered to introduce me to his partner and asked me for a copy of my business plan. Within 30 days, I had $1.5 million in capital investment to start my company.

Creating a Personal Advisory Board

Establish a network of subject matter experts (I used to call them my unofficial advisory board). I found there were many associates and leaders in my industry who were honored to provide advice and counsel. In some instances, they also found value in the collaboration of ideas. I remember being invited to serve on the National MBA Strategic Planning Committee in California. The meeting spanned two-and a half days with powerful leaders in the industry. At the time, I could not believe

I was sitting there with the elite group of leaders and statesmen of the mortgage banking industry.

After the meeting as I waited for a cab, Andy Woodward, Chairman of Bank of America Mortgage, was stepping up to his limo. He invited me to drive with him to the San Diego airport. I was flying to Philadelphia and he was flying to Charlotte, NC on US Air. At the airport, both of our flights were delayed. He asked if I wanted to wait in the US Air lounge with him. At the time, I did not even know what the US Air club and lounge was! We spent hours talking. He told me about his career, which included taking Bank of Boston and subsequently, Fleet Mortgage, public, as well as flying to Europe and all over the US presenting the initial public offering. Pretty impressive career.

He wanted to learn more about how I started my company and what it was like running an independent mortgage company not part of a huge bank. Of course, I thought my experience paled in comparison to his, but what was truly amazing to me is when he said, *"I envy you! I would give anything to build something from the ground floor and watch it grow."*

I won't labor the discussion except to say Andy became one of my biggest advocates in the industry, mentored me, and was MBA's chairman of the nominating committee the year I was nominated as chairman. There were countless times during my career Andy was there for guidance and counsel. In 2004, it was Andy who called to tell me I was nominated to be appointed the first female chairperson of the National Mortgage Bankers Association in its 94-year history.

It was one small step for me, but a giant leap for women, and carried the full weight of being a first. Although the nomination was unanimous, I was overwhelmed and, in some ways, felt inadequate. Not because I am a woman, but because this was the big league and I knew I would be under a microscope. It was then I decided to take the time out to pursue my CMB designation. At the time of my oral exam, prior to my inauguration as chairman, the proctors admitted they learned from me! Over the years, I have been recognized as an industry expert, called to testify before Congress, and advising other industry leaders and executives.

At the end of the day, finding the right supportive environment is key. Whether it is your family, friends, or mentors, it is important to have a network you can rely on to encourage and support you as you look ahead and forge a new path.

Building a Team

When Gateway Funding Diversified Mortgage Services was launched in 1994, conditions in the mortgage industry were challenging. Rates were rising and companies were stepping out of the business. I had no specific goal of breaking the glass ceiling, but after almost 10 years in the business, I was confident I could make it work. Having started with a small savings and loan in 1984, launching their mortgage business and rising through the ranks of senior and executive management, I knew the ins and outs of the business. It wouldn't be easy, but I was a workaholic with a vision, a strong sense of responsibility, and a plan.

We started with a team of seven employees. Having the right people in our tight circle was critical. This meant being brutally honest with myself about where I needed to build my bench strength and surrounding myself with talented professionals who believed in my plan. It meant choosing strong people and not being intimidated as they became leaders in executing my vision.

Developing this team did not happen overnight. Over the years, I learned to identify people who displayed certain inherent traits: purpose driven, team oriented, and self-awareness. Important lessons learned over my experience made me consistently and critically view the supporting team with the following:

Anyone can learn a skill or task, but did they have what it took to help grow the business?

Were they interested in learning the industry or learning their job?

Did they aspire to leadership, maybe even to be my successor, or simply to clock in and collect a paycheck?

Would they think about the bigger picture, improving the experience for everyone, or check off the boxes on their task list and wipe their hands of any additional involvement?

If they were a manager and had a challenge, did they have at least one recommendation for the solution?

I listened carefully to see how they described their success. The biggest giveaway was always whether they spoke using I or We descriptors.

Once I began building my team, I had to empower them. Being open with each other as a team in what can often be a tense environment is essential. Real estate agents and loan officers are on edge about meeting commitment and closing dates. Consumers are understandably anxious about what will likely be the biggest purchase of their lives which puts the pressure on agents and officers. Knowing there are 60 other loans in process helps to meter those expectations and leads to better decision making among the ranks.

Collaborative leadership is about relationships. The group had to feel comfortable speaking up, expressing their opinions, and offering their suggestions. As a rule, there were no silos. Differing viewpoints can be painful, but under the right leadership, conflict will always lead to broader consensus and growth.

INGREDIENTS FOR SUCCESS

Early in building Gateway, my biggest challenge was delegating responsibility. Any good leader has to delegate. I felt I had to have my hands in everything. Overcoming this trait was a big challenge for me. When overcoming the challenge of delegating responsibility, it moves you to a point where you can lead and surround yourself with other leaders and help them grow as leaders, too. In other words, I learned to collaborate with the team.

You also learn delegating responsibilities boosts confidence in your team. You soon learn you inspire others because they learn you value their ideas and there is no punishment. You create an atmosphere of trust.

In 1997, I was president of the Pennsylvania chapter of the Mortgage Bankers Association and on the board of the National Mortgage Bankers Association. Around the same time, there was an opportunity to acquire a competitor three times bigger than Gateway. We were a $50-million loan production business acquiring a $300-million loan production operation. With branches in New Jersey, Harrisburg, and Lancaster, this would allow us to expand our footprint. *The Philadelphia Business Journal* wrote, *"it was like a minnow trying to swallow a whale."* Even my partner did not think we could do it. I had to step out of my comfort zone again and take a huge risk; but we completed the deal through collaborative leadership.

We kept the owners on for a year. Learning from them helped with the transition and we were able to retain their team, folding them in to my team, and operating in different locations. It was a priority to make sure the cultures melded and became cohesive. Breaking down the silos between the Gateway team and the newly acquired team was critical to moving the goalposts.

Empower people with authority, trust, and accountability. We had become a $350-million loan production operation, with a five-year goal of hitting $500 million by 2002. It was a hell of a lot of hard work. There were challenges to growth: we had to continue to hire, and we had to maintain substantial warehouse lines of credit to fund the production and be sustainable. I was the catalyst to the team, rallying them together and empowering them to act as leaders. We collaborated on everything. As a rule, there were no silos.

At this point, the operation was too big to keep my hands on everything so the team had to be my eyes, ears, and advisors. They had to buy into my vision, and we had to be on the same page collaborating with one another. I had to let go and trust people. I had to delegate. One of the most immediately and consistently rewarding undertaking you can take as a leader is to empower your employees, while holding them accountable for the results of their decisions and actions. Management team leaders are motivated by trust and authority.

BE INNOVATIVE

We had to be innovative with incentives and make sure the people were being rewarded for their contributions to the team. Great salespeople tend to operate as mavericks, unconcerned with the minutiae, and as a result, often critical of the operations staff's dedication to procedure and detail. They want to hit hard and fast, and often take the operations staff for granted. The inverse is also often true, with complaints from the operations side about the recklessness of sales, but the truth is, without the dedication to collaborate from either side, we do not exist.

MILESTONES

The stars aligned for us as this strong team I built was able to take advantage of steadily decreasing interest rates. My networking led to partnerships with Fannie Mae and Freddie Mac. I joined their national advisory boards and became a partner with access as a direct lender. I grew Gateway Funding from seven employees to nearly 800 employees with 57 branches licensed to do business in 42 states.

As business surged, we did not stop to pat ourselves on the back. I built and led an all-hands-on-deck culture knocking our budget out of the park every month, and we didn't slow down as we pursued our goal.

Remember I said our goal was to hit $500 million by 2002. Well, we hit $500 million the middle of 2001 and we hit $1 billion in loan production in September 2001. A year and a half early!

And we didn't stop there. By the time I sold my interest in Gateway Funding in 2006, loan production was $3.5 billion, operating in 48 states.

NIGHT OF A BILLION STARS

This story isn't about growing Gateway Funding. It is really about the Billion Stars. All my experiences and lessons learned along my journey led to a Night of a Billion Stars, a celebration of our having reached the $1 billion mark. On this night, we cherished each star who bought into my vision and helped achieve it, not alone, but together, not as an island but as a community.

The Night of a Billion Stars was populated by those who took the time to listen and understand my vision. The team of people who made up those stars were mentors, partners, personnel, and friends who helped elevate each other so we could climb there together.

The journey to the Night of a Billion Stars has many lessons, including:

- Courageous Leadership—Learning to step out of your comfort zone.
- Learning to take risks and be confident in taking those risks. It's OK to fail. Learn from your mistakes.
- Learning to let go and delegate. Delegating empowers employees and it empowers you. Delegation also boosts morale and improves

efficiencies and productivity to help a company's bottom line.

- Learning to accept constructive criticism. Accept the criticism for what it is. It is a learning opportunity. Know when to step out of your own way.
- Listening. One of the most important skills to acquire is active listening. Really listen and gain an understanding of what you are being told.
- Watching.
- Communicating
  - Don't throw words at people. Communicate the vision and goals to motivate your team to achieve with efficiency.
  - Communicate clearly, enabling others to see what is expected of them.
- Building a collaborative network and contacts around you to include:
  - People who know more than you
  - People who are willing to challenge you
  - People who may not be friends but had a recipe to follow.
- Building a cross-functional team and empowering the team.
- Remembering you can build a great team but have bad leadership.
- Taking inventory of yourself. Know your strengths and weaknesses and be willing to learn how to be a strong leader.

*"Great leaders don't set out to be
a leader. They set out to make a
difference. It is never about the role,
it's always about the goal."*
~ Lisa Haisha

The Night of a Billion Stars was a red-carpet gala held in November 2001 celebrating everyone who contributed to our success. When I received the news the upcoming month's pipeline indicated we would be closing a billion dollars, I stepped back and realized I had built a team of stars. Every employee and partner was invited to be recognized and applauded. It was truly a celebration of the power of collaboration.

We hit a billion dollars because the team I built cared enough to make it happen. I had stepped out of my comfort zone and taken the risks, time and again, recruiting top-notch talent, making innovative decisions, and seizing opportunities for Gateway. I had used collaborative leadership at every level by networking to expand my professional reach, empowering my team to execute my vision, and taking a step back and delegating responsibility to people who believed in me.

It was the Night of a Billion Stars. The stars were visible and breathtaking to everyone who played their individual starring role.

I thank all my *Stars* wherever you are today! This story is about us—my vision, your hard work and devotion, your friendship and mutual respect.

We Made it Happen!

ABOUT THE AUTHOR

Regina M. Lowrie, CMB

IN A CAREER spanning more than 30 years, Regina Lowrie has gained renown as an inspiring leader, a highly successful senior executive, and a consummate expert in the mortgage and financial services industries. Her experience encompasses service as a C-suite executive in the banking industry, as well as many years spent exercising her entrepreneurial acumen as the founder of highly profitable private companies. She is recognized throughout the financial services industry for her comprehensive knowledge and experience in executive management with oversight of risk management, compliance, operations, capital markets, underwriting, sales and marketing, finance and information technology.

In addition to her accomplishments as a senior executive, Ms. Lowrie has extensive experience as an advisory board and board of director for a diverse list of public and private entities, including the Fannie Mae National Advisory Council, the Radian Guaranty Advisory Board, the board of directors of Cherry Hill Mortgage Investment Corporation (NYSE:CHMI), the board of trustees of Gwynedd-Mercy University, Montgomery County Community College and the Union League of Philadelphia board of directors.

Ms. Lowrie served as the first woman chairman of the Mortgage Bankers Association of America and holds a CMB designation. Throughout her career, she has been very active in the Mortgage Bankers Association at the local, state, and national level, as a member and elected official. Ms. Lowrie is also a highly sought-after speaker, who has delivered presentations on a range of topics to organizational events, including the Membership Meeting of the Federal Home Loan Bank of Pittsburgh and testimony before the U.S. Congress. She is the author of numerous financial services-related articles as well as an expert witness in the industry.

Ms. Lowrie is founder, president and chief executive officer of DYTRIX, Inc., a fintech company that serves the financial services industry. Ms. Lowrie developed a SOC-2 compliant technology platform that enables secure financial transactions that includes Closing Agent Management and Real-Time Wire/ACH transfer validation for institutions. The Dytrix Platform® is supported by secure and fully managed processes and a highly experienced team, mitigating the increasing risks of wire fraud and disclosure of non-public information.

Ms. Lowrie also serves as president and chief executive officer of RML Advisors, a consultancy firm she founded in 2007; providing the financial services industry with guidance on a broad range of services including vendor management, enterprise, regulatory, and compliance risk, and capital markets best execution, technology assessments and enhancements, and digital marketing development. RML Advisors also provides consultancy services relative to becoming a seller-servicer for Fannie Mae, Ginnie Mae, and other secondary mortgage market investors.

Earlier in her career, Ms. Lowrie was president of Vision Mortgage Capital, a division of Continental Bank, where she also served as senior vice president of the depository institution. In 1994, she founded Gateway Funding Diversified Mortgage Services and served as president and chief executive officer. During her tenure at Gateway Funding, she grew the company from seven employees and $1.5 million in capital to 800 employees with 57 branch offices licensed to do business in 42 states. When Ms. Lowrie sold her interest in Gateway Funding, loan production was $3.5 billion with revenues of more than $100 million.

Born and raised in Philadelphia, Ms. Lowrie has a longstanding commitment to being of service in Greater Philadelphia and other communities in the Tri-State area. Her involvement spans activities in a range of business-related organizations, such as the Greater Philadelphia Chamber of Commerce, The Forum of Executive Women and Credit Counseling Community Services of Delaware Valley. No less important to Ms. Lowrie is giving back to the community. She primarily focuses her philanthropic and volunteer efforts on education-related projects, which have included sponsorship of a golf tournament to raise scholarship funds for women students at Montgomery County Community College, and support of NewDay USA Foundation Scholarships at The Valley Forge Military Academy.

Career Highlights

- 2016 Fannie Mae publishes "Regina Lowrie: A Leading Force for Gender Equality in Mortgage Banking"
- 2013 Appointed State Ambassador under Mortgage Bankers Association State Ambassador Program
- 2005 First woman Chairman, Mortgage Bankers Association
- 2005 Certified Mortgage Banker (CMB) designation
- 2003 First female officer as 2004 Vice Chair-Elect of the Mortgage Bankers Association
- 2002 Elected Chair of the Residential Board of Governors, Mortgage Bankers Association.
- 2000 Appointed Chairman of MORPAC, Mortgage Bankers Association's political action group

- 1999 Gateway Funding becomes the region's 10th largest mortgage lender
- 1999 Gateway Funding a "Fastest Growing Private Company" in the Philadelphia Business Journal
- 1996 Appointed to the Mortgage Bankers Association Board and Executive Committee
- 1995 First woman to serve as President of MBA of Greater Philadelphia
- 1994 Elected Vice President of Pennsylvania Mortgage Bankers Association

Awards and Other Recognition

- 2020 Women in the Housing & Real Estate Ecosystem (NAWRB) Corporate Leader Award
- 2020 HousingWire's Woman of Influence Award
- 2019 Mortgage Banking's Most Powerful Women
- 2018 Mortgage Professional America – Hot 100 Leading Professionals
- 2016 Mortgage Professional America – Elite Women in Mortgage
- 2015 Cover story honoree of the inaugural issue of the Mortgage Women's Magazine
- 2014 The American Association for Women in Community Colleges Trustee of the Year Award
- 2014 Montgomery County Community College Leading Woman Award
- 2013 Mortgage Banking Leading Industry Women Honoree
- 2006 National Association of Women Business Owners' 2006 Women of Distinction Award.

- 2006 A Credit to Greater Philadelphia Community Award, CCC Services of Delaware Valley
- 2002 Mortgage Bankers Association of Greater Philadelphia Outstanding Achievement Award
- 2001 Mortgage Bankers Association of America's Burton Wood Legislative Service Award
- 2000 Honored by Governor Ridge as Pennsylvania's Best 50 Women in Business

Chapter 14:

The Road Less Traveled

Karen Deis

It was April 1, 1972.

All jokes aside, this was the day I started working in the mortgage business. For me, it is simply a great way to remember a pivotal day in my life. My whole business career has been about connections, about finding a need and filling it, and about making money each step of the way.

My story is about connecting the dots beginning with a receptionist job in a mortgage company which only lasted a few months. When the closing agent quit, I took his place. It was unheard of that a woman (in my mid-sized town) would be a closing agent and at first, there were real estate agents who did not want to work with me. They questioned my authority to hold funds if the closing conditions were not met. Complaints were made to my manager who, by the way, had my back, 100 percent.

Success comes when one finds a need and fills it. Making more money (because if you work 50-60 hours a week, you might as well make as much money as you can, right?) is a big part of the motivation, but it's not everything. As the first born of nine children, I remember always being in charge. I wanted to be a trailblazer. I knew when I was 17 years old I would be the president of my own company someday.

Before moving into the mortgage business, I was a purchasing agent. It may surprise you to realize how much being a purchasing agent prepared me for the mortgage business. There are many similarities, such as:

- Finding a supplier to buy is the same as finding clients or real estate agent referrals.
- Finding a product to buy is the same as finding money or wholesale investors.
- Finding the right price for the product is the same as shopping for rates.
- Having to track the shipment and make sure it arrived on time is the same as processing the loan.
- Ensuring the product is delivered with no damages and in the correct quantity is the same as closing the loan.

For the sales and marketing part, I learned from the salespeople who followed up with me, asking for more of my business.

Trailblazer from the Beginning

I never did any loan processing. I excelled at closing, however. My manager was correct to champion my right to the job. There was a lot to learn, of course. The closing documents must be perfect. I learned the importance of accuracy and the power of detail. The money needed to close must match the 1003. The money had to be wired. The proceeds of the loan must balance. The closing is usually where one finds the mistakes, ranging from loan officers (LOs) who did not complete the application properly to processors who did not read the documents or follow up on the conditions. I learned when there is money involved, people are emotional: they are happy, and they are upset. And I learned to negotiate with buyers, sellers, and real estate agents to close the deal.

The work involved in finding success as the first female closing agent turned out not to be a big deal for me. My path to becoming a loan officer (LO) was more challenging. As a closer, I found myself training male loan officers how to do their jobs correctly. They were being paid big bucks yet taking little responsibility for doing their job. I came to understand that no matter how good I was at my job the money was better on the front end. I broke fresh ground again when I asked to become a loan officer. At the time, there were no women loan officers in my town or company. I would again be first, assuming I was accepted. Resistance was high. I was told, *"Women don't work on commission,"* and *"Women need a steady income to support their husbands."*

DID YOU JUST SAY THAT?

I quit the mortgage company and found a job as a mortgage loan officer at a local bank. After a year capped by bringing in more business than my original company's LOs, I was recruited back to the mortgage company by my previous manager.

One day a competing mortgage company called and said to me, *"Karen, when you don't make it as a loan officer, I will hire you as our closing agent."*

I proved him wrong. As I connected the dots of my own career path, I also paved the road for others to follow. I was the first female loan officer, both at the bank and at the mortgage company.

Yet even as a successful LO, my trailblazing days continued. It had never crossed my mind there was a good old boys' network until I realized it was happening in my own company. A few years had passed during which time the company hired more women loan officers. Every year, the company had a party for all the men employees. I mean all the men, including the mail boy in the home office. I asked why women were not invited and was told the men played golf and poker. They smoked cigars and there was a lot of drinking.

What the hell? Women loan officers were instrumental in the profitability of the company and deserved to be recognized and rewarded. I organized a boycott. I asked my manager to boycott the annual event unless they allowed women to attend. I then called the managers of the branches where women LOs were employed and asked them to boycott the event, too. They all agreed.

216

Little did I know this would be a pivotal moment in my road to becoming a strong woman in the mortgage industry. The mortgage company president flew into town to have a talk with me. He explained why women were not invited. He threatened to fire me. I told him, *"Go ahead"* and assured him I would sue for discrimination. The annual event was changed, and the women loan officers were invited to attend.

A few years later, I became branch manager.

I learned a great deal from the experience. Stick to your guns! If you believe you are right, don't back down, even if it means you may lose your job.

To become a regional manager, I took a transfer to Houston, Texas. Here's the thing: this was during the oil crisis in the 80s and Houston was the epicenter. When I arrived there, I was told there was no business. Within seven days, I took my first loan application.

What did it take to write the application? I simply knew, somewhere in this big city, someone needed to buy a home. I just needed to find the right person. I started by talking to the real estate agents. With the agents, it's all about building trust and teaching them about the process so they understand I can close the loan and they will be paid their commission (yes, it goes back to the money motivation). It was tedious to find the one person. I decided to trailblaze again.

The mortgage industry was in a financial crisis in the mid-80s. The result, as in any similar crunch, was a higher number of foreclosures. HUD, at the time, sold the foreclosures to investors to move the properties off their books. I introduced a new concept to the Houston market

217

(pre-approval, which is the norm today), suggesting how files can be pre-underwritten and credit pulled to determine the client's buying power.

While I did not invent the concept, I convinced my company this was a unique way to secure clients and agents to do business with us. The foreknowledge of pre-approval allowed us to evaluate the chances for approval and increase our team's success rates. The percentages of final loan approvals were higher.

It is a complex dance, but here is a snapshot of how we did it. I started by reaching out to my connections, a couple of HUD officials I knew. We became one of their preferred lenders, complete with a booth at the auction. There was a large Asian-American community near our office, and I was one of the few loan officers who called on them. I mentioned the auction and advised our prospects to get in touch with their investors and bid on the properties. Asian investors were buying 15 to 20 properties at a time, which meant we closed 20 loans at a time. What I learned was to take advantage of the situation and create systems to make it happen.

After a few years, the new construction boom hit Houston. Since the investors bought the lower priced homes, there was a demand for more homes. The next step was to find a niche few loan officers were marketing to—working with builders. The problem was the person connecting had to be an approved lender. I got my foot in the door by presenting the pre-approved buyer concept: none of their other lenders were offering this. We became one of the recommended lenders for three of the largest builders in Houston.

218

This was trailblazing leadership and the risk paid off. Four years after arriving in Houston, we took the branch closing rankings from 103 to number eight. Our success was due to understanding the circumstances of the times we were in and being willing to step into the game as a player.

TAKE THE ROAD TO NEW OPPORTUNITIES

While I was building in Houston and honing new skills, my previous manager had become president of another mortgage company and wanted to specialize in new construction lending. He recruited me to move back to Indiana, to a town where the only person I knew was him. He was also president of the local home builders association and was acquiring business from custom builders but wanted to move into offering loans for tract builders. Using the same strategies I knew worked, such as preapprove buyers, discount fees, and create a follow up and closing system, we became the preferred lender for four tract-home builders.

But I was homesick.

Moving back to my hometown after nine years was challenging. While I still knew some of the real estate agents, 70 percent were new to me. Starting all over again (for the third time!), I relied on and modified my strategies for training new agents. My focus was on building alliances with builders and obtaining referrals from agents I had done business with in the past.

Was I trailblazing again? In a way, yes. I learned you can take what you created and modify it, then market it even if you don't know anyone in town.

I was in heaven; happily closing 15 to 20 loans a month.

Until a new branch manager was hired. I hate to say it, but SHE fired me. I was closing 15 to 20 loans while the other three male loan officers were closing two to three per month. She told me my loans in underwriting and closing would have to wait. The two to three loans the men closed had to come first because they needed to feed their families.

I became a raging bitch, and she fired me.

It was the best thing to ever happen to me. My dream of becoming a president of my own company was about to come true.

My sister Becky was the IT person for a large accounting firm. She was also studying to become a CPA. To be clear, I hate IT. I hate accounting. These professions are not my thing. I love sales. Marketing makes me happy. Being a trailblazer is awesome.

Becky and I were perfect business partners. As sisters, we got along with each other. Sure, we might fight and have different opinions. Those issues can be dealt with. Early on, we defined the roles we would each play within the company. We created a partnership agreement defining each of our roles. We built a business plan and included a buy-sell agreement in case things did not work out. This was in place before we started the company.

Here's a quick look at our business plan:
- Conventional conforming loans only.
- Offer pre-approvals (again, no one in my hometown was offering this in 1990).
- Focus on consumer-direct marketing.

- Focus on new construction business.
- Treat our employees like family.
- Make money.
- Invest 10 percent of gross income in stocks and bonds.

Each decision made was focused around those points.

Oh, and did I mention we were the first women-owned and all-women employee mortgage company in town? (We hired one guy who we had to fire for fraud!)

You know what I'm going to say right? Our competitors told people it would never work. They said mortgage brokers were scum (banks were the thing) and we would be bankrupt in six months because *women do not own mortgage companies.*

Within a year, we were the third largest lender, dollar volume wise, after the two largest banks in town.

There was one frustrating stumbling block. Focusing on consumer-direct marketing, I had a ton of leads to give to real estate agents. They took days to call the leads back, or they didn't call them back at all. The only solution I could see was to earn my real estate broker license and start our own real estate company.

First, we only originated conventional loans. Second, we provided full disclosure to our clients they did not have to use our real estate company, but quite a few of them did. The cool thing about the real estate company is we only represented buyers. We did not take listings, and the business plan was to specialize in just one thing and do it well.

We took 50-Did'tget getpercent commission and felt it was fair because the agents did not have to spend money to market. They did not spend money on desk fees or advertising. They were handed buyers, and each closed about 30 deals per year. They could shop other mortgage companies, especially for FHA, VA, or non-conforming buyers, but we still received 50 percent.

You might wonder, weren't the other real estate agents upset? Of course, they were. A couple of them called to tell us they would not be giving us any referrals. No loss. They never ever gave us any in the first place. Others who complained were those who we referred our clients to and took their sweet time to call them back. Again, no loss to us.

Remember, our business plan was consumer-direct marketing and we had control of the client.

While this cannot happen anymore, our state's regulation at the time was that one could also own an appraisal company if the owner was a real estate broker. To be clear, I was not an appraiser, nor did I play one on TV, but I hired a couple of the appraisers who worked for other companies and paid their expenses and a higher percentage per appraisal. Again, with full disclosure. Buyers could choose to use them or not (we did not discount the fees and charged the same as other appraisal firms) and we made sure our wholesale investors vetted them and accepted the arrangement. Our take was $100 per appraisal.

What we didn't realize at the time was this was the beginnings of one-stop shopping, which is the norm these days with real estate franchises and builders. Trailblazing without even realizing it. We saw an opportunity to fill a void, to correct a problem, and to create something unique.

DEVASTATING NEWS

Four years into owning the mortgage company, Becky was diagnosed with breast cancer. She was in and out of remission and it was evident she could no longer take the pressure.

Remember when I told you I hated IT and accounting? We decided to sell the company and this is where the buy-sell agreement became the blueprint on how we were going to divide the profits.

Becky was also a Master Gardener and with the profits from the sale of the mortgage company, she decided to start a nursery which would be passed on to her husband and children. She lived for another three years and fulfilled her dream before going to the big garden in the sky. The lesson I learned from Becky was you can use your experiences and knowledge to transition into your passions.

Another thing was happening at the same time in my life. My husband was offered an amazing job with a German manufacturing company that was setting up a division here in the US. We had to move to Wisconsin. He moved three times for me and my job and this was an opportunity for me to follow my passion—coaching and training loan originators.

This was the year 2000.

I was contacted by the publisher of *Mortgage Originator Magazine* (I was also a contributing editor) to hold live events featuring superstar loan officers who would share their sales and marketing ideas. It was called Mortgage Superstars and would include three speakers spending a half day at each event, traveling to 20 cities.

While there were other mortgage events out there, loan officers had to travel and take days away from the office. The advantage we offered was we traveled to their city instead.

It was a great three years on the road. After the program ended, companies would ask me how to reach the mortgage superstar loan officers because they wanted to hire them for their company events. The Mortgage Speakers Bureau was born. I would market them and be the booking agent, negotiate contracts and fees, and take a percentage of the speaking fee.

Remember when I told you I hated the technical side of running a business? I made the decision to hire an assistant to help me take my businesses to the next level. Jenna became both my right hand and left-hand person, working together for 18 years.

In 2002, *LoanOfficerMagazine*.com was born. Printed magazines where going away. The loan originators who had been writing for them wanted to continue writing and *Loan Officer Magazine* became the first online ezine in the mortgage industry. Yep. Still trailblazing.

In 2003, technology, specifically online videos, were in their infancy. I partnered with a tech guy to create online seminars while I worked with the speakers from the speakers' bureau to present sales and marketing ideas to the masses. While it cost us a bunch of money to create

224

the technology, our very first online seminar grossed $20,000.

In 2007 another good old boys' event happened. I was asked to be one of the featured speakers at a large mortgage event. What I did not know at the time was I would have been only one of two women to be on the main stage with 17 men speakers. What happened next was another pivotal moment on my road to making a change in the industry.

I received a phone call telling me I would no longer be on the main stage. I was replaced by one of his buddies. However, I would be part of breakout session consisting of all women. It was this moment when I decided I had enough of this crap. A few days before the event, I created a membership website called Mortgage Girlfriends where women could connect and network with each other. It was announced from the stage to give me their business card if they would be interested in joining. I received over 250 business cards and instinctively knew other women were tired of the good old boys' network, too.

I have since sold most of my subscription and membership websites to other mortgage women who, I am sure, will carry on my legacy.

Your Road to Success

I would like to end this chapter with a short outline of some of the lessons I learned as a loan originator and a woman business owner:

- Determine what your strengths are. Hire someone who likes to do what you don't want to do.

- Create systems for every aspect of your business. I recommend the book *The E-Myth* by Michael Gerber for inspiration.
- Know your competition and look for opportunities to fulfill a need not being pursued by others.
- Be true to yourself and your beliefs and do not let anyone tell you it cannot be done.
- Be brave when it comes to discrimination and harassment.
- When making a crucial decision about your business or your life, ask yourself, *"What's the worst thing that could happen to me?"* If you can live with the consequences, go ahead, and DO IT.
- Know your numbers. Create your own mini profit and loss statement because whether you realize it or not, you are self-employed.
- Save 10 percent of your gross income from every check you receive.

Finally, women tend to take care of others before taking care of themselves. It is going to be a hard transition, but if you do not take care of yourself first, you may become unhealthy and unable to help your family or be around to retire with a bunch of money.

Oh, and be sure to reward yourself periodically for being the awesome woman you are.

ABOUT THE AUTHOR

Karen Deis

No Shiny Objects: Marketing Basics Will Never Fail You.

It seems like every day, there's a new social media platform; a new phone app, an untested marketing idea, and everyone and their brother or sister is telling you about new ways to use them in your mortgage business.

But there are two problems with bright, shiny objects:

They make big promises that if you use this new idea or tool, you'll be wildly successful; and while bright shiny objects can be fun, they are also distracting.

To put it another way, it's like dressing yourself for work in the morning and adding accessories to what you are wearing now, but nothing matches your clothing.

This is where the basics will never fail you.

The ideas and strategies Karen has shared for years and years have worked for others. They are not the next shiny object. They are not rocket science. You may even think they are boring, but each one is designed to secure engagement (and leads) from real estate agents and consumers which is the name of the mortgage game these days.

"When I began in the mortgage business, I never imagined I'd become a pioneer and an advocate for women in the mortgage business. In my small town, I was the first woman closing agent, the first woman loan officer, the first woman branch manager, and ultimately the first women-owned mortgage company with an all-female staff. Since selling my company in 2000, I have advocated for women mortgage loans officers, coaching them on how to get more leads, close more loans and still have a life."

Karen started her mortgage career on April Fool's Day 1972. During her mortgage career, she was a closing agent, a loan officer, and a branch manager. In 1990, she started an all-women mortgage company, which became a one-stop shop for her clients. She also owned a real estate

228

company, an appraisal company, and she also co-owned a mortgage company with a large, tract builder.

In 2020, she sold several of her subscription and membership websites and created www.MortgageWomenSpeakers.com as a one-stop shop where mortgage and wholesale companies can hire successful mortgage women to speak at annual meetings, company events and virtual conferences.

Chapter 15

Idź dalej, bo możesz

Elizabeth Karwowski

Idz dalej, bo mozesz

Continue forward because you can

L et me take you back to a day when I met up with my old compatriot Mikey, a man I hadn't seen for years, from back in my Miami days. We had chosen a restaurant with an amazing patio and an ocean view for our tête-à-tête. Waiting for Mikey's arrival, I remember sitting on the patio wishing I was on vacation as I people watched tourists strolling the boardwalk. Lost in the moment, a tap on my shoulder brought me back to reality. This reality had a huge grin from a smile a mile wide. Mikey had arrived.

After pleasantries, it was catch-up time. It had been years since last we talked. Both of us had many stories to tell; stories I struggled with and felt embarrassed to share, while his seemed to be one adventure after another. While I was stressed out because of my business and a personal problem, he had been enjoying life as a screenwriter, sailor, and world traveler, had written his first book, and settled in to live on a tropical island. Our life journeys could not have been more different. As my friend Mikey was reaping the well-deserved benefits and success of his life, I faced professional ruin in mine.

I clearly remember the day years ago and the mixed emotions I felt after our reunion. Part of me was extremely happy for my friend Mikey and the lifestyle he lived, especially when I considered the contrast with mine. Mostly, though, I was mad, depressed, annoyed, and frustrated. After catching up with Mikey, I played every feeling back in my mind and for a long time those feelings didn't go away. Looking back, there were plenty of days and nights when I would throw my hands in the air and say, *"I'm done."* I said it more times than I can count.

As a first-generation ethnic Pole from Chicago, I was unable to turn to my parents for sage business advice because they had never experienced the challenges I faced. Their world was much different than mine when it came to running a business. What they did tell me, and I carry it with me even today, was idz dalej, bo mozesz (phonetic pronunciation: Eetch dahl-ay boh moshesh)

In English, it means continue forward because you can. Every time I was knocked down, took a hit, or struggled to stand back up, I remembered the great advice my parents gave, Idz dalej, bo mozesz.

HARD LESSONS TO LEARN

Words alone couldn't fix my problem. I had to do it. What fixed my problems was me taking control of my own emotions and not letting partners rule my destiny.

Have you ever faced a manager, an associate, or a partner whose actions affected you in ways you could not control? If so, I am especially glad you are reading this chapter to prepare yourself for the day you might. The rollercoaster ride of emotion, feeling you are out of control because of someone else's irrational thinking or action, can quickly turn you inside out.

While living in Miami, I reached a great intersection with my company: I had to decide how to grow the business to the next level. My choice was between staying in the industry we were in and trusting we would grow organically or bringing investors onboard to expand while embracing several opportunities. Investors were coming to me, asking me to partner. It felt as if I had arrived at a major turning point in my career. Being the main shareholder in the company, I made the decision to expand via the investor route, took the plunge, and ventured into brand new territory.

This made a drastic change in how I ran my business and presented a big learning curve to master. It was challenging to say the least. It was also exciting, maddening, and almost drove me into bankruptcy.

Looking back today, I don't think I made the right choice. I believe there was an easier route, I just didn't explore it. I should have explored other options. I was sold a bunch of BS and it sounded good. It's hard not to run with the excitement. New executives and young CEOs live off the excitement. It feeds their passion. It's how major mistakes are made.

Having lived through and barely survived my experience, I now have five major takeaways to share in hopes of helping to lessen your learning curve. Your path does not have to be as steep and challenging as mine. Follow the old chestnut, *"Don't do as I do. Do as I say."*

Lesson 1: Timelines and What If.

As my new partners and I moved through the start-up phase of our venture, individually we took on specific tasks that needed to be accomplished; at least I thought we did. As it turned out, I was a majority of one. Even though we had a plan, promises made were not promises kept.

In hindsight, I should not have ventured into the startup phase without having one major action completed. I made the mistake of failing to lockdown the timeline by drafting an inclusive due date. Somehow, I missed following through on the reason why I ventured into this partnership—controlling growth of the company.

Problems snowballed because we didn't have an agreed-upon timeline for actions and processes to happen. To add fuel to the mistake, we also neglected to create a backup plan to define What-If should the initial plan not happen.

In retrospect, this was not a good way to build a new business venture, although it was teaching me to become a better CEO.

Like building a home, you don't lift a hammer without having your finances in order. We couldn't hope to start and finish a project of this scope without a realistic timeline. Sometimes, because of unforeseen problems, timelines cannot be met. Always be clear as to why you are venturing into new territory and set easy-to-understand goals for everyone to accomplish.

If you don't, you will be stuck in the same space over and over again asking yourself why nothing is happening. As Einstein said, *"The definition of insanity is doing the same thing over and over again and expecting different results."*

Nothing comes from inertia. Talking is good, but NOT great. Reading it on paper is great as there can be no confusion when everyone is on the same page. If you are giving your time, your money, your list of clients (and more!), you must have a clear expectation of what your venture partners will be doing for you and WHEN. It keeps everyone focused as they should be.

Lesson 2: Failing to Plan is Planning to Fail.

A basic premise of business building as a leader and principle owner is to continually pose What-If questions and consider different scenarios around growth plans. The what-if lessons and questions I learned from building my original business were foreign to one of my more vocal partners. Whenever I asked a what-if question, his response was to marginalize the question (and by association me) saying, *"Of course we're going to do it."* He often punctuated the response with, *"Stop putting negative thoughts in your head, Elizabeth."*

This contrary and demeaning attitude from older, successful men around me fed into my own insecurities. After all, I was supposed to be learning from these mentors and I trusted their judgement. Problem was, they lied.

My gut kept telling me I needed a workable backup plan should my so-called partners fail to deliver on their promises. Days turned into weeks, weeks into months, and before I realized it, two years had passed. I had busted my derriere to promote and market our concept to potential customers.

We had estimated our so-called plan would cost seven figures to implement. I worked hard, making every effort to move forward, even though I had limited funds to do so. I met monthly with the executive team and still, funds were not being raised. The partners who brought the concept to me had one responsibility: to raise capital. It didn't happen.

I was a neophyte playing in a dirty environment and because I didn't know the rules, I paid the price. Every time I asked my partners for a progress update, they blamed the lack of accomplishment on one thing or another, never on their own inaction. At one point I was told I wasn't close enough to making deals and it was causing them to be ineffective. Mind you, all of us ventured into this new territory to raise capital. Finger-pointing came with comments like, *"The lack of success is your fault, Elizabeth."*

Failing to plan is planning to fail. This is another old adage and an important truth. I learned when we venture into a business with partners, especially an opportunity brought to you by someone else, make damn sure to have all their responsibilities laid out in writing, every last detail!

Lesson 3 Welcome a Good Support Team.

For quite a while nothing business wise slowed me down until I became pregnant again and my nanny told me she was returning to Poland. This information had the potential to be disastrous. The most difficult hire I ever made was finding the right nanny.

When my parents did not want to move from Chicago to Florida, it was a scramble. Time for my family to pick up, pack up, and move to Chicago where my parents lived to give Elizabeth some sanity support. Two months of packing boxes, takeout meals, making travel arrangements, and still running a business, and we were ready to go.

Then I had a miscarriage and had to deal with the physical, mental, and emotional complications I experienced from the unhappy event. In time, we pushed forward with our original plan and moved to Chicago.

Never had I considered the personal challenges I might face as I pursued my career and grew the business. I am truly blessed with a happy and rewarding family life supported by my husband, daughter, mother, and father. For me, good fortune was having this great support team, for my business and my personal life, as well. They picked me up when I was down and I am forever grateful for their love and support.

The lesson for you? Create a strong support platform to bolster you and share in picking up the pieces when unexpected events happen in life.

Lesson 4: Caveat Emptor.

Without a warranty, the buyer must take the risk is the basic meaning of the phrase caveat emptor. In the days when buying and selling was carried on in the local marketplace, this rule was practiced because the buyer and seller knew each other and were on equal footing. In modern days widespread commerce and technology places the buyer at a disadvantage. The principle remains true, however. It is a wise business owner who embraces the need for a caveat before entering into any partnership to avoid misinterpretation.

Do your research. When I say research, I don't mean on the surface. Understand the venture and what could happen if it fails. Plan for the worst and hope for the best. I didn't understand the absolute worst. This put me in the most vulnerable position among the partners because I had the most to lose in this venture.

Everyone else was able to walk away during the most difficult times, but I could not. I spent endless days and nights overseeing my normal responsibilities while learning a role I had no intentions or desire to learn. I ended up hiring multiple attorneys at the same time to resolve issues my previous partner did or did not do. My name was attached to everything. I couldn't walk away.

238

The financial repercussions of not doing my research early on and seeking out advice from the right attorneys cost me hard-earned money not to mention the time invested and emotional currency spent.

No one likes to spend money on attorneys when a venture is beginning. I understand. The question to ask and answer is, *"What will it cost you later to fix the unforeseen problems the attorney could have protected against?"*

When someone comes to you with an idea offering the opportunity to make money without spending money, question the premise. How and why can you spend money if you don't make money? Quickly, and I mean quickly, run the other way if someone says you can. Before you venture into territory you do not know, spend the 1K, 5K, even 10K to speak to an attorney who is an expert in the area you are venturing into.

I advise going even further. Speak to more than one; at least three, perhaps four attorney experts, if the option is available to you. No matter how expert they are in their field, each legal advisor is going to give you insights into your new venture coming from a different perspective with stories unique to each individual attorney's experience. The good news is they have nothing to win or lose by telling you the truth. By seeking out third-party advice you'll broaden your knowledge and gain the power needed to drive your destiny. As I have, you will learn A LOT from knowing the good and the bad.

Lesson 5: Lessons Learned the Hard Way.

Turning gray quickly does not mean you are seasoned. It means you experienced a lot of stress in a short period, at least it did for me. It's easy to say, *"Surround yourself with good, honest, and REAL team players who are not out to win for themselves."* It's more challenging to live the advice. It is also vitally important to your success.

When I was young, my parents didn't allow me to hang out with certain kids in the neighborhood. I thought those kids were having a lot of fun, doing cool things, and I wanted to be part of their fun. Seen through my parent's eyes, those kids were trouble. Obviously, we don't have our parents to tell us to avoid playing in certain business sandboxes. Will you avoid learning your lessons the hard way? Probably not. Perhaps though, you will avoid the stress and anxiety I faced by remembering the first four lessons I've provided here. I know I have learned those lessons well.

*****

When I finished my catch-up story with Mikey, he confirmed something I already knew and something I didn't. He said, *"And through all this, you got up and continued on. That's the Boss Lady I remember."* Without skipping a beat, he followed with, *"idz dalej, bo mozesz."*

Until that moment, I never knew he had a Polish background. These are the surprising moments making friendships and experiences in life so wonderful.

Through my emotional rollercoaster, his kind words, and the many words of wisdom my parents said to me, meant a lot. And with that, I say to you, "Continue forward, because you can." I'm happy to report the stories I tell during my next catch up with Mikey will surely be different and much easier to tell.

"Idz dalej, bo mozesz."

ABOUT THE AUTHOR

Elizabeth Karwowski

ELIZABETH KARWOWSKI IS the CEO of Get Credit Healthy, Inc, a technology platform that bridges the gap between the consumer and financial institutions, non-profit HUD counseling agencies, as well as any organization that relies on credit quality for their business decisions. GCH's technology is revolutionizing the remediation space with a simple, efficient, and cost–effective solution that integrates parties into one centralized platform providing business analytics to increase the number of consumers assisted day to day.

After graduating with honors from Northern Illinois University with a degree in Business Management, Elizabeth began her career in the financial world with Ernst & Young and RSM MCGladrey. In 2004, she left to start her own mortgage company, Trust One Mortgage Corporation. Viewing the mortgage industry through the lens of a broker allowed Elizabeth to observe the pain points of both lenders and the consumers, which prompted her to develop GCH360, the platform on which Get Credit Healthy operates.

As a recognized credit expert, Elizabeth has been featured on NBC and Fox News, and published in *Scotsman's Guide* and *Today's Chicago Women*, to name a few. She received her FICO & Fair Credit Reporting Act certifications from the Consumer Data Industry Association in 2009. Due to her passion and persistence to make a difference, Elizabeth and her company are now collaborating with Fannie Mae to help borrowers gain essential knowledge to prepare for sustainable homeownership.

Elizabeth has also received Progress and Lending Innovation award, was named One of Mortgage Banking's Most Powerful Women 2019 from NMP, 2020 NAWRB Consumer Advocate Leader Award, and a proud recipient of the Women With Vision Award in 2019 and 2020. She built her company from the ground up and is making major inroads in the lending space.